A Guide to Ancient Maya Ruins

A GUIDE
TO ANCIENT
MAYA RUINS

by
C. Bruce
Hunter

University of Oklahoma Press   Norman

Library of Congress Cataloging in Publication Data

Hunter, C   Bruce.
    A guide to ancient Maya ruins.

    Bibliography: p.
    1. Mayas—Antiquities.   2. Mexico—Antiquities.
3. Central America—Antiquities.   I. Title.
F1435.H86   917.2'03   74-5956
ISBN 0-8061-1214-X
ISBN 0-8061-1215-8 (pbk.)

Preface

This book was written for the traveler who wishes to explore some of the great Maya ceremonial centers. Thus the sites included here are those that can be reached by the traveler, even though some are in remote regions.

For more than a century and a quarter the magnificent ruins of the Mayan civilization in the jungles and highlands of Mesoamerica have excited the imagination and curiosity of people all over the world. Once only the most intrepid of explorers and scientists, traveling by muleback or on foot, hacking their way through the jungle with machetes, could see for themselves the remnants of that once-great civilization. Today, however, with the building of roads and bridges and air fields, a number of important and impressive sites can be visited by the tourist.

In the twenty years that I have been leading field-study trips to these archaeological zones for the American Museum of Natural History, I have seen the number of travelers increase manyfold. In these years it has become apparent that an adequate guide to the accessible ruins and the means of getting to them is needed. In this book I have tried to fill those needs.

Descriptions, explanations, and appraisals of Maya structures and works of art have been provided. Each site is set in its historical period and identified by location, topography, external influences, and internal motivations as well as they may be surmised at this time. I have tried to reconstruct Maya life to bring the great pyramid temples and sweeping plazas into focus as centers of bustling activity, far different from the mysterious and forbidding monuments that they seemed to their discoverers.

Because this book is primarily for the traveler, I have not included some Maya centers regardless of importance—such as Uaxactún, Piedras Negras, Altar de Sacrificios, and many other ruins in the Petén, Río Bec, and other areas—that either have not been restored or are extremely difficult to reach.

If A Guide to Ancient Maya Ruins can help the traveler decide which archaeological zones to visit, if it can make his trip more enjoyable and what he sees more comprehensible, then my purpose in preparing it has been accomplished.

In accumulating the data for this manuscript, I am indebted to the writings of Maya scholars from the time of John L. Stephens to the present day. In particular, I would like to mention William Coe, George Kubler, J. M. Longyear, Samuel Lothrop, Sylvanus G. Morley, Tatiana Proskouriakoff, Alberto Ruz, Albert Spinden, and J. Eric S. Thompson. I am especially grateful to Gordon Ekholm for reading the manuscript and making valuable suggestions. Christopher Schuberth was most helpful in clarifying geological phenomena unfamiliar to me. I would like to thank Judy Miles and Gloria Davis for their suggestions and kind assistance in preparing the manuscript. I am grateful to David Jones in Hawaii and Jack Steiger and Jim Wood in Amagansett, who placed their homes at my disposal for the writing of this manuscript. I wish to thank Gail Hunter and Laurie Carrico for their secretarial assistance.

C. BRUCE HUNTER

New York City
March 20, 1974

Contents

Preface   *page* v

I   Introduction   3

II   The Pacific Slope
      Monte Alto—El Baúl—Las Ilusiones   24

III   The Petén
      Tikal   40

IV   The Motagua River Basin
      Copán   74
      Quiriguá   112

V   Lower Usumacinta River
      Palenque   126
      Yaxchilán   158
      Bonampak   168

VI   Pasión River
      Seibal   179

VII   Guatemala Highlands
      Kaminaljuyú—Zaculeu—Nebaj   191
      Mixco Viejo   206
      Iximché   213

VIII The Puuc Hills
      Uxmal   221
      Kabah—Sayil—Xlapak—Labná   256

IX   Northern Yucatán
      Chichén Itzá   276

X   Quintana Roo
       Tulúm   305
Suggestions for Reaching Archaeological Zones   319
Organized Tours   321
A Word About Clothing   321
Selected Readings   323
Index   325

Black-and-White Illustrations

Corbeled Arches	*pages* 13
Maya Glyphs	15
Boulder sculpture, Pacific slope	25
Boulder sculpture, Pacific slope	26
Boulder sculpture, Pacific slope	28
Monumental sculpture, Cotzumalhuapa style	30
Bas-relief, Cotzumalhuapa style	32
Carved column, Cotzumalhuapa style	34
Carved head, Cotzumalhuapa style	36
Temple I (Temple of the Giant Jaguar), Tikal	44
North Acropolis, Tikal	46
Rain-god mask, stucco, Tikal	48
Great Plaza, Tikal	50
Stela showing Maya dress, Tikal	53
Stela (detail), Tikal	54
Great Plaza, Tikal	56
Temple II (Temple of the Masks), Tikal	58
Rain god, stucco on wood, Tikal	61
Temple III (Temple of the Jaguar Priest), Tikal	62
Central Acropolis, Tikal	64
Stela and altar, Tikal	68
Corbeled vault, Tikal	71
Stela and altar seen through corbeled arch, Tikal	72
Facial detail, Stela C, Copán	78
Stela C, figure on east face, and Stela B, Copán	79
Stela A, front, Copán	80
Detail, Stela B, Copán	81

Stela A, back, Copán   83
Detail, Stela A, Copán   84
Stela H, Copán   86
Hieroglyphic inscription, Stela D, Copán   87
Stela C, figure on west face, and turtle altar, Copán   89
Altar G, Copán   91
Stela F, back, Copán   93
Stela J, Copán   94
Ball Court, Copán   96
Hieroglyphic Stairway, Copán   99
Figure on Reviewing Stand stairway, Copán   101
Sculptured head, Copán   103
Altar Q, Copán   104
Detail, Jaguar Stairway, Copán   107
Doorway, Temple 22, Copán   108
Figure stela, Copán   109
Sculptured heads, Copán   111
Stela E, Quiriguá   118
Zoomorph P, Quiriguá   123
Drawing of Zoomorph   123
Aerial view of Palenque   130
Palace, Palenque   132
Stucco sculpture, Palace, Palenque   136
Stucco sculpture, Palace, Palenque   137
Detail, stucco sculpture, Palace, Palenque   138
East Court, Palace, Palenque   140
Bas-relief, Palenque   142
Detail, bas-relief, Palenque   143
Temple of the Inscriptions, Palenque   146
Drawing of Temple of the Inscriptions   147
Temple of the Sun, Palenque   151
Temple of the Cross, Temple of the Foliated Cross,
    and Temple of the Sun, Palenque   152

Oratory-type structure, Palenque 157
Usumacinta River 159
Detail, stone sculpture, Yaxchilán 163
Structure 33, Yaxchilán 165
Hieroglyphic panel, Yaxchilán 167
Plaza area, Bonampak 169
Detail, Stela 1, Bonampak 173
Stela 2, Bonampak 175
Detail, Stela 2, Bonampak 176
Structure 1, Bonampak 177
Sayaxché ferry across Pasión River 181
Structure A-3, Seibal 182
Stela 9, Seibal 186
Stela at Sayaxché 187
Stela 2, Seibal 189
Mounds, Kaminaljuyú 192
Structure 1, Zaculeu 197
Structure 13, Zaculeu 199
Narrative painting on Mayan pottery 200
Carved jade from Toniná 205
Site of Mixco Viejo 209
Ball court, Mixco Viejo 211
Pyramid C-1, Mixco Viejo 212
Building remains, Iximché 218
Ball court, Iximché 219
Great plaza area, Uxmal 224
House of the Magician, east façade, Uxmal 227
House of the Magician, west façade, Uxmal 228
Nunnery Quadrangle, Uxmal 230
Drawing of Nunnery Quadrangle, Uxmal 232
North Building, Nunnery Quadrangle, Uxmal 234
Mosaic decoration, Nunnery, Uxmal 236
Rain-god-masks façade, Nunnery, Uxmal 238

East Building, Nunnery Quadrangle, Uxmal 240
West Building, Nunnery Quadrangle, Uxmal 242
Detail, mosaic decoration, Nunnery, Uxmal 243
House of the Doves, Uxmal 244
Rain-god mask, Grand Pyramid, Uxmal 247
House of the Turtles, Uxmal 248
Detail, cornice molding, House of the
  Turtles, Uxmal 249
House of the Governor, Uxmal 250
Corbeled arch, House of the Governor, Uxmal 252
Detail, House of the Governor, Uxmal 253
Mosaic decoration, House of the Governor, Uxmal 254
Arch, Kabah 257
Palace of the Masks, Kabah 258
Detail, Palace of the Masks, Kabah 260
Palace, Sayil 262
Detail, Palace, Sayil 263
Detail, Palace, Sayil 264
Restored structure, Xlapak 266
Palace, Labná 268
Second story of Palace, Labná 270
Detail of carving, Palace, Labná 271
Detail of carving, Palace, Labná 272
Castillo, Labná 273
Vault, Labná 274
Castillo, Chichén Itzá 279
Ball court, Chichén Itzá 280
Detail of carving, Tzompantli, Chichén Itzá 285
Detail of carving, Tzompantli, Chichén Itzá 286
Detail of carving, Main Plaza, Chichén Itzá 288
Sacred Cenote (Well of Sacrifice), Chichén Itzá 290
Temple of the Warriors, Chichén Itzá 291

Detail of carving, Temple of the Warriors,
    Chichén Itzá   292
Red House, Chichén Itzá   297
Observatory (Caracol), Chichén Itzá   298
Nunnery, Chichén Itzá   300
Iglesia, Chichén Itzá   303
Aerial view of Tulúm   306
Temple of the Frescoes, Tulúm   313
Detail of mural, Temple of the Frescoes, Tulúm   314
Castillo, Tulúm   317

*Unless otherwise credited, all photographs
were made by the author.*

Color Plates

Stela B at Copán   *following page* 110
"Altar" at Copán
Monumental Sculpture at Copán
Toniná Jade
Great Plaza and North Acropolis of Tikal
Temple III, Tikal
Stucco Portrait
Maya in Ceremonial Clothing
Sculpture from East Court, Palenque
Stela from Sayaxché, Guatemala
Temple of the Inscriptions, Palenque
Structure 41, Yaxchilán
Structure 5, Yaxchilán
Palace of the Masks, Kabah
Palace at Sayil
Palace at Labná
Labná Arch (Vault)
House of the Magician, Uxmal
Detail from Quadrangle, Uxmal
Tulúm
The Observatory at Chichén Itzá
East Annex of Nunnery, Chichén Itzá
The Castillo at Chichén Itzá

Maps and Site Plans

Mesoamerica	*page*	4
Maya Area		8
Maya Ceremonial Centers		9
Southern Maya Area		27
Pacific Coast *Fincas* and Archaeological Sites		35
Tikal		42
Copán		75
Quiriguá		113
Palenque		128
Yaxchilán		160
Bonampak		170
Seibal, Southern Section of Group A		180
Zaculeu		195
Mixco Viejo		207
Iximché		214
Uxmal		222
Chichén Itzá		277
Tulúm		308

A Guide to Ancient Maya Ruins

I   Introduction

The first movement of peoples from the Asiatic mainland to the Americas, the mode of transportation, and the reason for leaving their homeland is still somewhat of a mystery. A northern land bridge between the two continents made it possible for easy immigration between 25,000 and 9000 B.C. This bridge was to disappear when the depth of the sea rose to approximately 350 feet during the Wisconsin deglaciation. During this time the movement of peoples along the coastal waters and overland into the Americas was rapid. By 10,000 B.C., these peoples, organized into small hunting and fishing bands, had populated the Americas as far south as Tierra del Fuego.

Sometime between 5000 and 2000 B.C. the domestication of fruits and vegetables was begun, and many of the hunting and fishing groups settled into a more sedentary life in hamlets, and agriculture became the basis of economy. By 1500 B.C. the Maya region was well populated, as were many other regions in Mesoamerica.

The first two major civilizations to emerge in the Americas were on two separate continents. In South America, during the Middle Preclassic Period (1200–400 B.C.) a dominant culture developed in Peru, now known as Chavín. Remains of the stone structures from this time are still visible today at what is believed to have been its capital, Chavín de Huantar. In Mesoamerica, the culture contemporary to Chavín was that of the Olmecs, located in the coastal region of Veracruz. Both civilizations were to influence other peo-

3

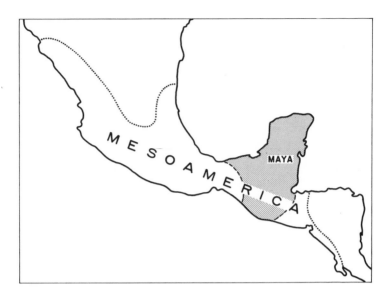

Approximate Extent of Mesoamerica

ples in farflung areas. At the time these two important civilizations came to an end, a sprinkling of other cultures were
on the ascendancy in both South America and in Mesoamerica.

In Mesoamerica, as early as 600 B.C. the Mayas were already organized into cultural groups. Even at this time the
area of the now-famous ruins of Tikal was occupied by the
Mayas. Between 600 B.C. and A.D. 250 great activity in city
planning was taking place all over Mesoamerica. Cultural
areas were being defined. Ceremonial centers were constructed, trade routes and trade luxury goods fostered trade
competition between regions, and the sciences of mathematics and astronomy as well as writing were the concern of
the academicians of the time.

During the Classic Period, which started as early as A.D. 250 in some areas and ended as late as A.D. 900 in others, Mesoamerica reached a florescence in cultural development never to be equaled again. In Mexico the greatest of the Classic civilizations was Teotihuacán. Its capital site, located approximately thirty miles north of Mexico City, had a population somewhere between fifty thousand and one hundred thousand persons—a city much larger than most European cities of that time. The influence of Teotihuacán was felt throughout all of Mesoamerica. Other important cultural areas in Mexico during the Classic Period were Monte Albán, which was under the control of the Zapotecs, the area of Cholula, and Classic Veracruz. On the southern end of Mesoamerica during Classic times, the Mayas dominated the whole area of Yucatán, the southern part of Mexico, all of Guatemala, Honduras, Belize, and El Salvador. Their influence was extraordinary, affecting cultures from Costa Rica to the Mexican highlands.

Europe was well entrenched in the Dark Ages, most of Africa was little known even to the Mediterranean world, India and China were in their Golden Age with the ascendancy of the Gupta and Tang dynasties, when the Mayas were blossoming into the greatest of all civilizations in the New World. Maya scientists had accomplished feats in astronomy and mathematics not equaled by their contemporaries in the Old World. Accomplishments in the arts had reached a sophistication comparable to any other great traditional culture in the world.

At the ceremonial center of Palenque, delicate stucco reliefs decorated the beautiful façades of temple and palace buildings. Tikal architects designed and constructed the tallest of all pyramid temples in the heart of the Petén jungle. Copán was the most southerly of the larger Maya cities,

5

and the scientists there startled their contemporaries with their developments in astronomy. Architects at ceremonial centers in the Puuc Hills of northern Yucatán created masterpieces in stone mosaic as decoration for their splendid "palaces." Wall paintings, some in true fresco style, adorned the temples and other structures throughout the land, creating a brilliance in the tropical sun that could only astound those persons paying homage at the ceremonial centers. The brilliance of the color of the frescoes at Bonampak, now over one thousand years old, hint at the excellence of art throughout Mayan civilization.

Maya territory extended from El Salvador and Honduras into Guatemala and Belize, north to the Yucatán Peninsula, and west as far as Tabasco and Chiapas. It would seem the territory was divided into city-states, controlled by ruling families who may have been both political and religious leaders of their realms. The organization of the social structure and all of its attendant activities was also in their hands. Dedicatory statues in the form of stelae are located at many ceremonial centers, and recent research by Tatiana Proskouriakoff on genealogies of Mayan monuments suggests that the rulers may have been considered to have divine power. The Mayan civilization, seemingly at peace with the world, matured for approximately fifteen hundred years, developing in arts and sciences without interruption. After reaching a Classic florescence that lasted some six hundred years (A.D. 300–900), the civilization reached a hiatus. Many cities were abandoned, the arts declined rapidly, and foreign control or influence was apparent. In the Guatemala highlands the Mayas shifted their cities and towns to hilltop locations where they could be fortified. However, with the arrival of the Spaniards it was obvious that never again would the Mayas have a chance to rise as a world civilization.

6

For many years writers sought ways to explain the "great mystery" of the Mayan collapse. All civilizations seemingly must go through the cycle of beginning, flowering, and ending, and the Mayas were no exception, although they enjoyed an unduly long civilization in comparison to other cultures in the New World. The Incas, Toltecs, and Aztecs lasted fewer than five hundred years. Of the many writers who have offered explanations for the Mayan collapse, J. Eric S. Thompson, in *Maya History and Religion*, gives us perhaps the most plausible explanations of the Mayas' downfall. In brief, the Maya political and religious system, during Late Classic times, was beginning to erode. Local cult deities and household gods were gaining appeal as opposed to the pantheon of gods used at the large ceremonial centers by the old priestly and ruling classes. Also, the hamlets administered by local rulers were pressing for more autonomy as their communities increased in size to larger towns and cities. The labor required to construct the great ceremonial centers was a tremendous drain on the energy of the laboring class of people in these smaller hamlets. Revolt or abandonment of the entire area was inevitable. Mutilated sculptures indicate revolt in at least one ceremonial center. At the time the Maya ruling chiefs were having problems with their own cities, groups of militant people from the Valley of Mexico and the Gulf states kept pushing farther into the Mayan area. Some Maya cities came under the control of these foreign peoples during Middle Classic times causing trade disruption, social unrest, and agricultural difficulties. Such people as the Nahuatized Pipils interrupted the calm of the Maya world by introducing their militant attitudes, secular ideas, pantheon of new deities, and art style influenced by El Tajín and Teotihuacán. New iconographic details became quite evident on Late Classic sculpture. This is especially noted at

7

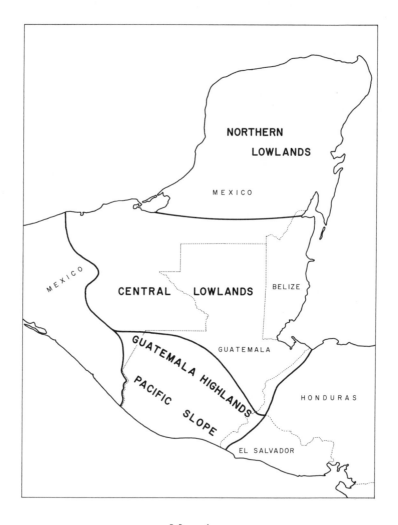

Maya Area

DZIBILCHALTÚN

CHICHÉN ITZÁ

MAYAPÁN

UXMAL
KABAH
SAYIL LABNÁ
YAXUNÁ
COBÁ

JAINA
TULÚM
Cozumel
Island

EDZNA

HOCHOB

XPUHIL
RÍO BEC

COMALCALCO
Río Candelaria

Río Usumacinta
ALTUN HA

Río Grijalva

PALENQUE
UAXACTÚN
TIKAL

PIEDRAS NEGRAS

TONINÁ
BONAMPAK
YAXCHILÁN

ALTAR DE SACRIFICIOS
Río Pasión
SEIBAL

Río Salinas

RATINLIXUL
Lago
de Isabal

ZACULEU
NEBAJ
CHAMÁ

Río Ulúa

QUIRIGUÁ

MIXCO VIEJO
Río Motagua
COPÁN

IXIMCHÉ
KAMINALJUYÚ

EL BÁUL

MONTE ALTO

0   50   100 Miles

Maya Ceremonial Centers

Seibal and Altar de Sacrificios on the Pasión River. Other Maya ceremonial centers were completely abandoned without indication of further occupation. The jungle quickly recaptured its hold on the territory, snarling it in a network of lush tropical growth—buried for another thousand years, when archaeologists and adventurers were to discover ruins in America.

The Maya territory is divided into three major areas: the highlands bordering the Guatemala and El Salvador Pacific slope, the central lowlands stretching along the Usumacinta River basin through the Petén to Honduras, and the northern lowlands including the whole area of the Yucatán Peninsula. Rulers of Maya city-states were autonomous, but they did enjoy intercommunication and co-operation throughout the vast territory. Archaeological excavations at most of the major ceremonial centers indicate that there was an exchange of a wealth of knowledge from one Mayan region to another on such subjects as writing, religion, achievements in the arts, and achievements in science. Even beyond the Maya borders, influence was felt from the Classic Veracruz area, the Zapotec region in the Valley of Oaxaca, and the Izapa style that persisted along the Pacific slope and into the Guatemala highlands. The great civilization of Teotihuacán, in the Valley of Mexico, was also to leave a strong cultural influence in the Maya area, especially at Tikal and Kaminaljuyú.

Because of the long historical progression of expanding activities in ceremonial centers, the demand for exotic produce from foreign territories, and the need for communication and co-operation between the various city-states, transportation and trade routes became an important and integral part of Mayan cultural development. The lords, priests, and scientists had constant need to communicate with each other. Architects and sculptors certainly engaged in a lively exchange of ideas and were instrumental in fostering competitive activities in the ceremonial centers. The position of the merchants was also important enough that they may well have been members of ruling families. Rivers and the sea became the great highways for the Mayas. Rafts and canoes, some with sails, were used for transportation on these waters. Paved highways also served as important communication links from one area to another, such as those between Kabah and Uxmal, and from Cobá to Yaxuná. Footpaths through the jungle were also used, and on some of these one might see a body of retainers composed of servants and advisers accompanying a lord, priest, or merchant in a wooden litter. Narrative scenes on pottery and wall murals depict such movements through the jungles.

Except for metals natural resources were abundant in the Mayan territory. Much of Petén and the Yucatán Peninsula rests on a bed of limestone which yields no metals. However, limestone was extremely important as a building material for the cities and towns. It was also important as a carving stone for monuments. Sandstone and andesite were sometimes used where limestone was not available. Flint, jade, and obsidian were fashioned into important trade items. Jade was especially valuable and was considered much more precious than any other single item that one could own.

The basis of the economy was agriculture. In the area of the Guatemala highlands the soil was especially fertile. Corn was the main crop, but other produce was grown, especially beans, squash, peppers, and tomatoes. Cacao, a luxury for the rich, was grown along the Pacific slope, in British Honduras, and in Chiapas and Tabasco. Harvest from fruit trees, such as the breadnut, plum, papaya, guava, and coconut, was also accessible. The forest was a valuable source for much necessary produce for the home and building projects, rubber for the ball game, resin for religious ceremonies, barks and leaves for making paper, and dyes.

In the Maya territory slash-and-burn agriculture was practiced, and this system is still being used today. Once the land was cleared by burning, it was then possible to plant crops. The northern lowland area has a porous limestone base in which water cannot be retained. Because of the dryness of the land, a scrub-bush type of environment is present. Except where a system of irrigation was practiced, utilizing water from cisterns and *cenotes*, the yield in agricultural produce was very sparse.

The Maya civilization had its early beginnings around 600 B.C. From that time we have indications of templelike structures surrounded by other buildings located in various sectors of the Maya area. By Late Preclassic times (300 B.C.–A.D. 250), such ceremonial centers as Uaxactún and Tikal in the Petén were using stone for building and for the carving of fine monuments. Stucco decoration was in vogue at Tikal during this time and visitors can see large stucco mask forms on buildings in the North Acropolis at Tikal today. At this early time ceremonial centers were already the nucleus of the Maya community. Plazas were designed to enhance the temples. Palace buildings and houses for important personages were built around a series of courtyards. Early temple buildings were laid on rectangular stone platforms or low stepped pyramids. The actual temples, during Preclassic times, were constructed of perishable materials, but post holes on the tops of these platforms indicate their size and type of construction. This early type of community planning set the pattern for the great ceremonial centers built during the Classic Period (A.D. 300–900).

Dwelling houses of the Mayas today show little change

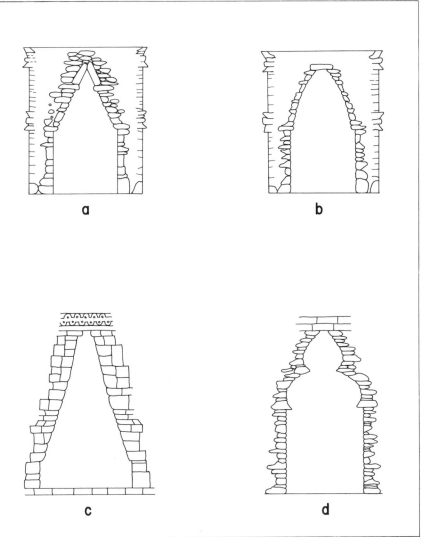

Corbeled Arches: The Mayas were ingenious in the many ways they constructed the corbeled vault. These four types are only a sampling of the great variety of doorways used. a. Nunnery, Chichén Itzá; b. Uaxactún, showing curved soffit slopes; c. Uxmal, entrance to Palace of the Governor; d. trilobate arch, Palenque Palace. (After Sylvanus G. Morley, The Ancient Maya)

from those built two thousand years ago. From the beginning houses were extremely functional. The high roof of thatch and the thick adobe side walls insured a cool place in which to live in an environment that was extremely hot and humid.

The corbeled vault, so much a part of Maya architecture during Classic times, was an obvious outgrowth of the high peaked roofs used by these people from earliest times. Vaulted entrances to plazas and patios, vaulted arches to cities, and vaulted rooms and porticoed chambers were a prominent feature of Maya architecture. Excavations to date have not revealed the use of a true keystone. Methods of vaulting are highly varied to accommodate the shape of the arch or door. Also, there are many regional differences in the way stones were cut for vaulting. At Palenque the use of the trilobate arch presented a difficult problem for the Maya craftsmen. At Uxmal the stonecutters employed interlocking shaped stones to strengthen the arch. The northern lowlands also commonly used a boot-shaped stone to strengthen the larger doorways. These structural stones were then covered over with a thin veneer of mosaic stones that became a part of the exterior decoration of the building cornice.

A system of recording in hieroglyphics had its beginnings outside of the Maya area, possibly as early as Middle Preclassic times (800–300 B.C.). Early glyphs can be seen on monuments at Olmec sites in Tabasco and Veracruz. Monte Albán is another area where the recording of dates and inscribing of glyphs, as yet undecipherable, were performed at a very early time. The Mayas used some of these rudimentary glyphs, but developed many other glyph forms until their system of writing became the most advanced in the Americas. Their symbols for glyphs are a combination of ideographic representations mixed with abstract or abbrevi-

Maya Glyphs. Top: Head variant glyphs for the number eight. The Mayan artists had many ways of expressing the same number. A bar and three dots also expressed the same number. Full-figure glyphs were also used. The great number of variations for numbers and words has added to the problem of deciphering the Maya script. Center, left: A full-figure glyph for Baktun time period. The head variant is a bird. Stela D, Copán. Center, right: A full-figure glyph for Tun time period. The head variant is attached to a serpent's body. Hieroglyphic Stairway, Copán. Bottom: Glyphs may also be grouped as phrases; this one is from Tikal. (From J. Eric S. Thompson, Maya Hieroglyphic Writing: An Introduction*)*

ated representational forms. It is quite possible that some parts of glyphs may represent syllables.

A glyph consists of several component parts: a main glyph form with associated smaller forms that may be affixes representing adjectives, adverbs, and other modifying factors. Sometimes two glyphs are combined to form a single block, thus altering the meaning of the individual glyphs. Many variant glyph forms were used for the main symbol of a glyph. This has complicated the deciphering. For instance, a numeral may be represented by dots and dashes, by a head variant, or by a full-figure variant. Scholars concerned with research on Maya glyphs are slowly unraveling this cumbersome system of writing. Although less than half of the glyphs have been deciphered to date, much information has been gained from them in regard to the Maya knowledge of astronomy, calendrics, gods, and ceremonies.

Monuments such as stelae and altars were being carved during Preclassic times and became extremely important during the Classic Period at such ceremonial centers as Copán, Quiriguá, Tikal, and Piedras Negras. On these monuments are finely carved glyphs commemorating events that had taken place. The Mayas had an obsession with carving dedicatory monuments. At some centers stelae were erected at five-year intervals. Other centers observed the ten- or twenty-year interval for erecting stelae. Most stelae have associated "altars." These altars were really additional commemorative monuments that probably did not serve as altars, but may have been used strictly as decorative carvings for the great plazas. In some instances they may have been used for offerings, such as flowers, fruit, or other food, that would honor the gods.

The Mayas carved very large panels of glyphs as decoration for their buildings, and the largest of these can be seen at Palenque. The longest of all hieroglyphic inscriptions is placed on the facing of the beautiful Hieroglyphic Stairway at Copán. There are glyphs on stairways throughout the Maya territory. Hieroglyphic inscriptions carved in stone have been found at more than ninety archaeological sites. Mayans recorded much of their history, scientific discoveries, and religious data in books. Unfortunately, the damp tropical forests were devastating to this fragile type of material. The Spanish conquerors destroyed most of the Maya literature they could find. Today, there are only three Mayan books, or codices, surviving—all in European collections.

Eight hundred years of Preclassic cultural development set the stage for the Maya Classic florescence. Sometime between A.D. 250 and 300 a new surge of activity permeated the great ceremonial centers. Architects were finding new ways to build greater palaces and temples—much more complex than those in Preclassic times. Architectural detail showed new refinements in the relationship of one tectonic member to another; in the clean, crisp method of cutting stone; and in the exquisite expression of the human figure in stucco relief on piers, walls, and roof combs of buildings. New techniques in stone mosaic, for decorating the façades of temples and palaces, were also introduced during the Late Classic Period. Buildings were plastered and painted at various times throughout Mayan history. Wall paintings, in brilliant colors, decorated both the exterior and interior of structures.

Much has been written on the dark, dismal, small rooms in temples and palaces that are damp and not suited for human habitation. These assumptions are based on modern Western standards and on observations at ceremonial centers as they are today. In the thousand years since their abandonment, mosses, lichens, and algae have encrusted buildings and monuments at the ceremonial centers, and the encroaching growth of tropical forests has enveloped them, causing dampness and disintegration. During Classic times the forests were kept cut back, and the plazas, courtyards, and buildings were completely plastered with fine lime and painted. With the abundance of labor, this type of maintenance was continuous at the ceremonial centers. As an example, the interior of Temple 22 at Copán was covered with twenty-five coats of plaster. Walls were also painted in brilliant hues of green, yellow, orange, red, and blue that made them glisten in the sunlight. With this type of preservation, the interiors of rooms were dry, bright, and cheerful. The need for a number of different types of rooms for habitation, in terms of modern standards, does not apply to the Maya style of living. Its glory and prestige did not lie in the number and furnishings of rooms but in the public ceremonies and festivals. Temple and palace rooms must have been for multiple use. Sitting, eating, and sleeping could easily be arranged in a single room, much as it is in Mayan houses today. Archaeological evidence, in scenes on wall murals and pottery, would indicate very sparse furnishings. The many benches in temples and palaces seem to imply that these were used for sitting and sleeping, while the recessed areas served as storage places for blankets, cushions, and portable tables. Traditionally, cooking facilities were always kept apart from living quarters by the Mayas.

With the emergence of the Classic Period, ceramic pottery took on new shapes, and vases were painted with polychrome decorations—narrative scenes depicting the lords of the Maya realm, a pantheon of Mayan deities, animals, and glyphic inscriptions. A number of the most superb painted vases, with handsomely executed brush strokes, were made at Ratinlixul and Chamá, little-known sites to the north of the

Guatemala highlands. However, there was extensive production of ceramic ware throughout the Maya area.

Some of the most magnificent jade pieces were carved during Late Classic times (A.D. 600–900). The largest carving found to date came from a recent excavation at Altun Ha in Belize (formerly British Honduras). This amazingly large carved head weighs nine and three-quarters pounds. Carved figures and animal forms are rare in Mayan jade. An unusual carving, discovered during excavations at Tikal, is that of a crouching jaguar weighing three and one-half pounds. Most jade was carved as ornamentation for the ruling families and priests. Important merchants would also wear jade. Some of the carving is extremely delicate and certainly tested the skill of the lapidary, as his tools for shaping, grinding, and polishing were of stone or bone. Some of the finest jade carvings, and the most numerous, have been found in the Guatemala highlands at the sites of Kaminaljuyú and Nebaj. Another source of Maya jades has been the *cenote* at Chichén Itzá. Two of the most important burials in the Americas, in which great quantities of carved jade were discovered, are at Tikal (Burial 116) and in the Temple of the Inscriptions at Palenque—the famous tomb discovered by Alberto Ruz Lhuillier.

Many new discoveries in the sciences, such as methods of computing the moons and the tropical year, were announced from the Copán center. Information such as this was quickly passed on to other Mayan centers. The spirit of co-operation in endeavors of science, religion, building programs, and festival ceremonies are evident throughout the Maya area. Hieroglyphic texts, stylistic influences, and religious homogeneity would indicate that a degree of peace and tranquillity existed between the various city-states. One can assume border skirmishes at times. The Bonampak murals well illustrate the type of raid one village may have made on another, and its effect.

Ceremonial centers were constantly being enlarged during various time cycles. A new building program was often inaugurated at the death of a great ruler, the ascendancy of a new lord, the discovery of a new computation in astronomy, or the birth of a new deity. Sometimes new ceremonial centers were constructed, sometimes old centers enlarged. For the most part, the architects were more apt to build a much larger building over an existing structure. When this was done, the area around the walls of the existing building would be filled in with rubble, and often the original structure would be left intact—much to the advantage of future archaeologists. Superimposition of this type continued throughout Mayan history. It is not unusual to find many superimpositions in a single structure. For instance, the House of the Magician at Uxmal has five superimpositions and the North Acropolis at Tikal has over a dozen earlier versions under it. Mesoamerica is unique in the world of archaeology in this particular type of architectural construction.

Considering the amount of activity carried on at a large ceremonial center, there must have existed many schools and training centers for youth. The sons of the elite had to master reading and writing, learn the achievements in science and the arts, study architecture, know mathematics, memorize the rituals of religious practice, and know the laws and mores of society. Training schools were needed for apprentices in other occupations such as scribes, accountants, merchants, masons, weavers, lapidaries, sculptors, painters, actors, dancers, and musicians. Many of these occupations formed a basis for additional social groupings and created a bridge between

the elite and the laboring class. Thus, the Maya social structure was not a two-class status society, but had varying levels
of social groupings according to skills and knowledge needed
for occupational specialization. Many of the occupations
were inherited—not too unlike the way craft guilds operated
in medieval Europe. Mobility in Mayan society, from one
status to another, would not seem to have been an easy
matter.

Little is known of Maya religion during Classic times.
However, the codices, monuments, temples, and pottery
give us some idea of the pantheon of gods and their importance. Scholars have relied on such sources as Bishop
Landa's *Relación de las cosas de Yucatán*, the *Popul Vuh*,
and *Annals of the Cakchiquels* for information on Maya religion during the Late Postclassic Period. Generally speak-
ing, the greater number of Mayan gods were concerned with
the forces of nature and had dual identities. They represented good or evil, male or female, animal or human or a
combination of both forms, and presided over night or day.
This type of multiplicity, together with the changing nature
of the gods over the long history of the Mayas, makes it difficult to reconstruct the general pattern of their religion.
Many of the gods were linked to the cardinal points and were
associated with various colors.

Some of the gods served several purposes and had changing functions and forms, as in the case of Chac, the rain
god. He was a reigning deity of winds, and sometimes was
depicted with symbols of death. The young maize god, Yum
Kaax, who became so important at the site of Copán, was
also the embodiment of the ideal in male beauty. He served
an additional function as protector of newly married couples.
Ah Puch, the god of death and lord of the underworld, was
also the malevolent god of the Mayas. He opposed fertility

21

and was often accompanied by animals of ill omen, the owl, *moan* bird, and dog. Another important deity was Itzamná, the sky god, who had many attributes but was usually depicted as a toothless old man with sunken cheeks and a hooked nose. His wife, Ixchel, was the moon goddess and protector of women in childbirth. At the time of Cortés' landing on the island of Cozumel, the shrine for this goddess was one of the most popular shrines along the Quintana Roo coast. Other important gods were Kinich Ahau, the sun god; Xanam Ik, god of the North Star; and Ek Chuah, the war god.

The complication of the Maya pantheon of gods becomes more so when they can be related to the Mayan cosmos. The thirteen heavens and nine underworlds, all ruled by sky deities, and lords of the night were also ritualistically significant in Mayan calendrics. Afterlife was an important concept of the Mayas' religion, and apparently most persons expected to go to paradise. Ceremonials accompanied by fasting and feasts certainly were an integral part of life at the ceremonial centers. Religious rituals, cycles, and ceremonies perpetuated by lords and priests became a great fascination, inspiration, and ensnaring bondage for the masses of people who labored to build the tallest of all pyramid temples in the world.

The character of Mayan ceremonial centers showed marked changes during the Postclassic Period (A.D. 900–1500). Because of political unrest, Mexican migrations into the Maya area, and the emergence of new city-states with a new ruling class, ceremonial centers became more secular in character, fortified, and militant. These changes can be seen in such Maya cities as Tulúm on the east coast of Quintana Roo, at Mayapán in Yucatán, and in the Guatemala highlands at Iximché and Mixco Viejo. In the six hundred years of Postclassic development, there is not one Maya ceremonial center that has any of the grandeur, the excellence of workmanship, or the accomplishments in the sciences or arts as did those of the Classic Period.

With the entrance of the Spanish conquistadors, the Maya people were to witness the complete destruction of their literature, religion, and great works of art and to see the decimation of their people by warfare and disease.

II   The Pacific Slope
Monte Alto–El Baúl–
Las Ilusiones

Pantaleón, El Bilbao, Los Tarros, Monte Alto, Las Ilusiones
—names that now take on new meaning to the townspeople
along the coastal plain of the Pacific. These large property
holdings, called *fincas*, are yielding some of the more recent
archaeological finds from the systematic excavations of the
scientists. Sugar-cane fields and coffee plantations along the
Pacific slope of Guatemala, only hours south of Guatemala
City, are still holding some of the great archaeological treasures far beneath the surface soil. A great number of large
boulder-type sculptures have been uncovered at Finca Monte
Alto and other neighboring *fincas*. One of the large heads
was found at the Finca El Transito by two children. As in so
many of these sculptures, the eyes are closed, lips are full,
ears are long, and face is round. In these heads the sculptor
expresses an energetic inner force enhanced by the simplicity
of the sculptural line. Many of these sculptures represent the
heads or whole figures of plump, chubby persons. They have
been found in association with ancient mounds that must be
the remains of very old ceremonial centers that served religious purposes. Future excavations here may give us a clearer idea as to the size and configuration of these early ceremonial centers and how they functioned.

For many decades these carved boulders have been appearing along the Pacific slope as far south as El Salvador.
The Kaminaljuyú site in Guatemala City has also yielded
many stones carved in this same style. The figures on the
boulder sculpture are characterized by a barrel-like body, a

Large heads without bodies comprise the most common type of boulder sculpture along the Pacific slope. Their purpose and their exact dating is unknown. Such boulder sculptures as these are reminiscent of the monumental stone sculptures carved by the Olmecs during Preclassic times. This head type usually has puffy lips, a bald head, and closed eyes. The stone is a dark gray basalt. Late Preclassic.

baby face that usually has closed eyes, arms and legs that are simplified to ribbonlike bands wrapping around the obese figure, sex undifferentiated, and nudity or scant clothing. The carving is executed with a minimum of sculptural planes, and the back of the boulder is usually not carved at all. On

Large boulder-type sculptures are found over a large part of the Pacific slope, and into the Guatemala highlands. Many of the stones have been moved into the park at the village of La Democracia from the surrounding fincas where they were discovered. In this sculpture the general shape of the boulder is obvious. The man is lying on his back, and the legs and arms are indicated by "wrap-around" planes that show little detail. Monument 2 was found at Monte Alto. Late Preclassic.

some stones the ears, nose, and eyes are little more than line etchings, while other areas of the boulder are in high relief. A dark gray volcanic stone, basalt, is found in natural boulder form on the terrain and is utilized for these carvings.

Southern Maya Area

Olmec sites in Veracruz and Tabasco have been credited with the earliest monumental sculpture in Mesoamerica. These centers are located at La Venta, Tres Zapotes, and San Lorenzo. Their sculpture is characterized by its monumental size, sophisticated carving techniques, and simplicity of form. Many of the heads and altars of the Olmecs are much larger than any of those located on the Pacific slope of Guatemala. As we study the Olmec culture, there seems to be little indication of any rudimentary beginnings to their monumental artistic accomplishments. It is quite possible that this earlier

27

A number of the boulder sculptures have been discovered on the
Finca Monte Alto. Adjacent fincas such as El Transito and Nuevo
are also known for this type of sculpture. The face of this head
(Monument 3 from Monte Alto) has suggestions of a feline deity
more often associated with Olmec sculpture. Late Preclassic.

period of their development is associated with some of the archaeological materials now slowly being uncovered along the Pacific coast of Guatemala. However, much more research has to be undertaken before any critical analysis can be made.

Most archaeologists concede that the boulder sculptures in the Monte Alto area are very old. The sculptures were at first placed in a vague Late Preclassic stage that allowed a latitude of time for stylistic changes. However, it is plausible that some of these sculptures could have been carved earlier. Edwin Shook's most recent research on the monumental stone carvings would suggest an approximate date of 300 B.C. to zero A.D.

A number of the monolithic stones from Monte Alto have been moved to the village square in the little town of La Democracía, a most arbitrary and unbecoming location. A little museum in this village houses other early stone carvings that are smaller in size.

The next important stylistic influence to affect the Pacific slope was from Izapa, a small ceremonial center just north of this region in Mexico. Izapa is the type site for this style, although the origin may have been in the Veracruz area. During Late Preclassic and Proto Classic times (300 B.C.–A.D. 300), this style was to influence the whole southern end of Mexico, the Pacific slope of Guatemala, and the highlands at Kaminaljuyú. The style has some Olmec traits such as scrollwork skies or clouds, the flame-scroll brow, St. Andrews-cross motif, and scenes framed by a jaguar's jaw. However, characteristics strictly Izapan appear, such as deities descending from the sky, winged figures, U-shaped symbols, and the long-lipped god.

The Izapa site was abandoned at the end of Late Preclassic times, but the beauty of the style was to influence

Monument 28, located at Finca Las Ilusiones, is one of many sculptures adjacent to the finca headquarters. Not far from here is the location of the Cotzumalhuapa site that is believed to be Late Classic.

Classic Maya sculpture, especially at Tikal. The next major influence on the Pacific slope of Guatemala and as far south as Honduras and El Salvador was from Mexico. During the Middle and Late Classic periods (A.D. 400–900), invading or migratory Pipil-speaking peoples from the central highlands and Veracruz occupied the area. This Pipil-Nahuatized people were imbued with the Classic culture from El Tajín and Teotihuacán. In particular the Fincas Las Ilusiones, El Bilbao, El Baúl, Panteleón, Los Tarros, El Castillo, and Santa Rita were to feel the major effect of this last major stylistic influence. Lee Parsons, who has been carrying out archaeological research along the Guatemala slope, refers to this style as Cotzumalhuapa. The style is characterized by speech scrolls, non-Mayan glyphs, ball game players in association with death manikins, sun disks, sky deities, and human sacrifice.

A few miles north of Monte Alto is the site of El Baúl. Today there is little indication of the old ceremonial center. The earliest of the sculptures have been removed to the nearby village, where they can be seen in a little park. Sculptures include heads of men, mythological beings, deities, and a variety of animal forms. These decorative elements may have enhanced panels in walls, cornices, moldings, door jambs, or lintels. Large carved figures have shanks that would suggest they were tenoned into the walls. These sculptures are carved in the Cotzumalhuapa style.

The earliest dated stela, Monument 1, to be discovered in the Mayan area is located here, with a dedication date of A.D. 36. (The earliest non-Mayan dated stela [Stela C] found so far is located at Tres Zapotes and it has a dedication date of 31 B.C.). Monument 1 is carved in the Izapa style. There is much Preclassic pottery and sculpture on all the surround-

Monument 30 is located in the town of El Baúl. This is only one of a number of similar types of sculpture. The style of the carving and the glyphs are associated with the Nahuatized-Pipil

culture, active toward the end of the Late Classic Period. The style is referred to as Cotzumalhuapa.

Monument 13 at El Baúl suggests a portraiture of a bearded person. Heads of this type may have been tenoned into the façades of buildings as decoration. Lee Parsons has carried out field work in this general area in the hope of establishing a chronology. Middle to Late Classic.

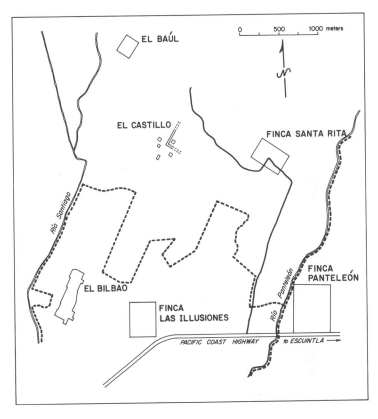

Pacific Coast Fincas *and Archaeological Sites*
(after Parsons)

ing *fincas*. However, the Cotzumalhuapa sculpture of Middle and Late Classic periods is predominant.

Most of the Cotzumalhuapa-styled sculptures are found at the Fincas Las Ilusiones and El Bilbao. These plantations have coffee as their chief crop, but in recent years sugar cane has also been grown. Even cacao, at one time economically important, is still grown here. The area is heavy in rainfall,

35

Monument 3, located in a sugar-cane field not far from El Baúl, is a type of monumental sculpture that may have been introduced by the Pipil-speaking migrants who moved into the Pacific slope area during Middle and Late Classic times. The wrinkled brow is reminiscent of Plumbate effigy jars that appeared in the Guatemala highlands in the Early Postclassic Period. Today the sculpture serves as an altar for local cult worship.

creating a tropical growth, lush and exuberant. Many of the sculptures and other artifacts at El Bilbao have been removed from the major site area, Monument Court, to the headquarters of the *finca*, owned by José Ricardo Muñoz Gálvez. In its early history this *finca* was known as Bilbao, a name used for the title of the two-volume manuscript on the archaeology of the Pacific slope written by Lee Parsons. Bilbao is also the name used for the type site encompassing the entire area.

On the *finca* El Baúl, locally referred to as Finca San Francisco, there are still two very large monumental sculptures in the Cotzumalhuapa style hidden away in a clump of trees surrounded by a sugar-cane plantation. One of these heads, Monument 3, is that of a wrinkled old man. Today the Indian populace uses this monument as a shrine. It is not unusual to see a soothsayer there saying prayers while he swings an incensory that is smoking with copal. Offerings of flowers and sometimes chicken eggs, which are broken over the stone, are left.

In the year 1880 a very important group of Late Classic stone monuments, numbering over thirty pieces, were removed from the *finca* El Bilbao. They were all carved in the Cotzumalhuapa style. Eight of the monuments are the famous Cotzumalhuapa stelae. After five years of arduous labor in transporting the sculptures to the coast, they were shipped to Germany and now are housed in the Volkerkunde Museum in Berlin. The eight large stelae are the finest carved monuments of their type from the Pacific slope. Unfortunately, one of the stela was lost in the ocean when it was being transferred from the shore to the ship. Guatemala lost many of its great art treasures when explorers and adventurers carted them off around the turn of the century. The illegal robbing of mounds for artifacts is still going on today in both Mexico and Central America.

The Cotzumalhuapa stelae show decided Mexican influence in the use of speech scrolls and other symbolic motifs not associated with the Mayas. The carvings, in low relief, depict ritual scenes associated with ball-game ceremonies, with similarities to carvings at El Tajín. The monuments were taken from the Sunken Court where the ball court is located. The site has produced no superstructures for the court, so commonly used by the Mayas throughout the highland and lowland regions. In the museum in Guatemala City replicas now can be seen of two of these Cotzumalhuapa monuments.

Mushroom-shaped stones, as well as *metates*, mortars, and other stone objects, have frequently been dug up on the *fincas* while the fields were being prepared. The carving of mushroom stones, in a variety of sizes and styles, started in Preclassic times, possibly as early as 500–300 B.C., and continued into the Postclassic Period (A.D. 900–1200). The earliest types can be identified by a groove around the top. This type, carved during Preclassic times, may also have a stem that is carved with an effigy figure, and the base of the mushroom may be a tripod or a square. During Classic times the mushroom had no groove, and the stem was plain. This was the general style pattern, but it was marked by regional differences.

In Kaminaljuyú nine *metates* and *manos* were found with nine mushroom stones dating to the Miraflores stage (300 B.C.–A.D. 150). This number suggests a relationship of the mushroom stones and *metates* with the nine Lords of the Night or Underworld, as depicted in Mayan art and mythology.

Mushroom-shaped stones are found in the Mayan area along the Pacific slope, in the Guatemala highlands, and in the eastern lowlands as far south as El Salvador. From the Spanish chronicles we know that mushrooms were used for various types of ritual ceremonies among the Aztecs, Mixtecs, Tarascans, and other groups in the Mexican highlands. The hallucinogenic mushrooms were ground on a *metate*, water was added, and the mixture was drunk for specific cult rituals. Stone mushrooms have not been found where these present-day cults exist. We are not certain that these stones were representations of mushrooms. They may have represented the phallus or had some other meaning.

No significant superstructures of ancient ceremonial centers are visible in the area of the Pacific Slope today. The greatest number of mounds, seventeen in all, is located on the *finca* El Bilbao. There is little known regarding these mounds and the significance in ancient times of the structures they cover.

Continued archaeological excavations and research along the Pacific Slope should unfold more of the developmental stage of the three major art styles and the ceremonial centers with which they were associated.

III The Petén
Tikal

Above the two hundred-foot-high mahogany, cedar, and chicle trees that screen the Petén jungle from the air appear the five great roof combs on the pyramids at Tikal, piercing the crest of the green tropical forest. The landing field for the plane is adjacent to the Tikal Museum and the Jungle Lodge. The Jungle Lodge, the only place to stay while at Tikal, is an interesting experience in communal living. Antonio Ortiz is in command of operations here. He runs the lodge, transports the guests, arranges air passage, and is one of the most informed persons to guide visitors through the ruins of Tikal. However, with the excellent manual written by William R. Coe, *Tikal: A Handbook of the Ancient Maya Ruins*, it is possible to see Tikal on your own, provided you have a few days to relax and explore the many trails that meander through some of the more remote regions of the forest. Both the howler and spider monkeys sweep through the jungle in mid-afternoon just behind the Central Acropolis. Their noise can be heard for miles. Keel-billed toucans, motmots, and parrots are some of the many birds that give color to the jungle environment. In the early afternoon, the air is clear, the trails in shadow, and the temperature comfortable to explore the remains of this once great ceremonial center and the surrounding area, a thriving city over a thousand years ago.

Tikal was an active area as early as Preclassic times (600 B.C.–A.D. 250). Ecologists believe that the Petén jungle may have been savannah country even as late as Classic times.

The area became the dense jungle forest it is today after its abandonment. In part, this environmental change may have been due to climatic shifts. At its height, during the Late Classic Period (A.D. 600–900), Tikal had a dispersed population of approximately fifty thousand people. Tikal and Teotihuacán were the two largest urban centers in Mesoamerica during Classic times. Today the area of Tikal is a national park, covering 222 square miles, for the preservation of the archaeological zone.

Tikal is a site that had been known since the seventeenth century. Alfred Maudslay's detailed drawings of Tikal, executed in 1881–82, alerted adventurers and scholars to the possible wealth of the Tikal ruins. Teobert Maler explored and photographed the area both in 1895 and 1904. Earlier than this, the Swiss gentleman, Gustav Bernoulli, visited the area and had the lintels removed from Temples I and IV; these are now in the museum in Basel, Switzerland. Sylvanus G. Morley made many trips into the Petén between 1914 and 1928, and his scholarly contributions on Maya inscriptions are a monumental achievement.

It was the year 1956 that the University of Pennsylvania inaugurated a bold and dramatic program for Tikal in which some of the major buildings would be excavated and partially reconstructed. Thirteen years later, 1969, their great work here was concluded. Only a fraction of the area has been restored. Even so, the work involved was not too dissimilar from rebuilding a Maya city. The great care needed to excavate such an important zone as this can be appreciated only by watching the archaeologists at work, sifting every teaspoon of dirt over acres of land as they slowly piece together the remains of Mayan history. As we see the ruins of Tikal today, they are a monument not only to the Mayas who originally built them but also to the many scholars who

41

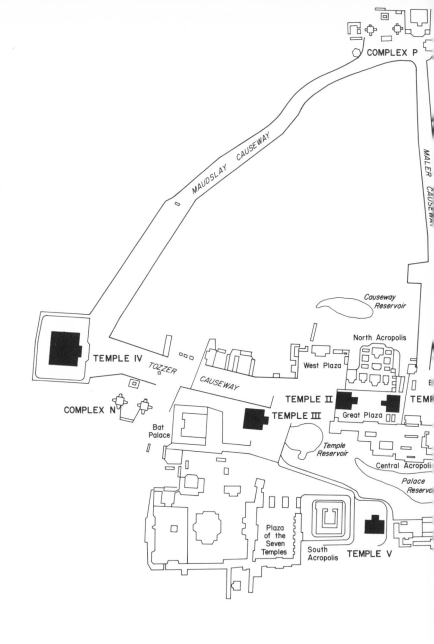

Tikal

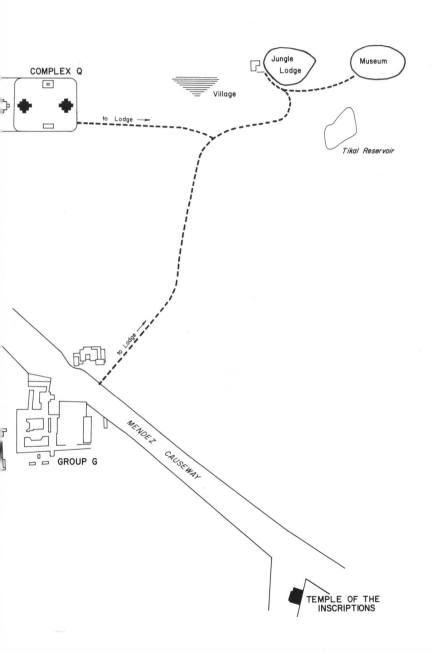

COMPLEX Q

Village

Jungle Lodge

Museum

to Lodge →

Tikal Reservoir

to Lodge →

GROUP G

MENDEZ CAUSEWAY

TEMPLE OF THE
INSCRIPTIONS

*Temple I is one of six major temple pyramids at Tikal. The tall-
est here is Temple IV, which towers 229 feet above ground level.
Temple I, also known as the Temple of the Giant Jaguar, faces
the Great Plaza. It was constructed about* A.D. 700.

worked here during these years to restore a small part of the splendor that was once the great city of Tikal.

The five great pyramids of Tikal, rising into the sky above the forest ceiling, give this ceremonial center a majestic grandeur unlike other Mayan cities. The height of the temples, the complicated assemblage of the palace structures of the Central Acropolis, and the complexity of the chronology of the North Acropolis are staggering to anyone first visiting Tikal. The main function of Tikal was that of a ceremonial center in which the aristocratic elite and their priests ruled, dictated, and directed the activities of the architects, builders, craftsmen, and laborers. All endeavors within the territorial area of Tikal were directed to enhance the city, to glorify the gods, and to amass wealth for the ruling upper strata of society. This was a continuum to last for over a thousand years that could have been sustained only with a well-disciplined peasantry. The highest pyramid in the New World is Temple IV, in which the roof comb is 229 feet above ground level. Approaching the Great Plaza, the impression is one of monumental scale. Temples I and II face each other from the ends of the plaza. The palace buildings are to the south, and the extraordinary North Acropolis looms over the whole expanse of the ceremonial center.

Excavations in the North Acropolis proved exceedingly fruitful in revealing the early history of Tikal. Earliest structures that mark the beginning of the ceremonial center, excavated at the lowest level of the North Acropolis, are Preclassic buildings dating back to 200 B.C. This dating indicates a long developmental period for the Mayas at Tikal before the Early Classic Period commenced in A.D. 250. During this long period of time the acropolis went through innumerable changes. Early structures in this area were mostly temples. The style of architecture was already showing refinements,

45

The North Acropolis can be best viewed from the top of Templ
I. Construction started in the North Acropolis in Preclassi

*times and continued through the Late Classic Period. The struc-
tures seen here today date from the Early Classic Period.* 47

In the North Acropolis at Tikal are several Early Classic buildings with stucco decoration. This huge rain-god mask decorates part of the façade of Structure 5D-sub.

such as apron moldings that would eventually evolve into the Classic style. Over the next six hundred years the North Acropolis was built over many times, being enlarged until it covered two and one-half acres. Under this huge complex is buried the long history of past generations and each of their architectural accomplishments. Stucco decoration was used on some of the earliest buildings here, and, of course, throughout Mesoamerican history most buildings and monuments were painted in brilliant colors. With constant razing, enlarging, and adding of new structures, the network of old buildings under the present plaza floor became a maze of architectural superimpositions. From the North Acropolis a striking view of the Great Plaza is seen, stretching into the distant jungle. Rising above the horizon is Temple V, second tallest pyramid at Tikal, which towers 188 feet above ground level. Unrestored, the temple roof comb is covered by a lush green carpet of ferns, mosses, and tropical shrubs.

The lofty roof combs at Tikal are the most massive of any in the Maya area. The Tikal architects did not pierce the roof comb, a common practice at other ceremonial centers such as Palenque, Uxmal, and Yaxchilán. The exterior of the roof comb is a solid mass, but the interior has a partially hollow core that is vaulted and sealed. This lessens the weight of the comb on the temple walls. The tremendous weight of the comb made it necessary to build extremely heavy supporting walls, leaving little room for the actual temple. Stucco decoration, in the form of heroic masks, was added to the front panel of the roof comb. This panel was then painted.

Although the Mayan architects did not plan completely symmetrical buildings or for that matter symmetrical ceremonial centers, at Tikal there is a greater suggestion of formal relationship of one building to another within the plazas, and especially within the twin-pyramid-complex compounds.

The Great Plaza, stretching over two acres, has had four superimpositions of plaster over a period of six hundred years. Construction of the plaza started as early as 150 B.C. William R. Coe, who directed so much of the work at Tikal during its reconstruction and excavation, estimates that the last resurfacing of the plaza was completed in approximately A.D. 700.

The north end of the plaza is dotted with stelae and

49

51

The Great Plaza at Tikal. Temple I is on the left and the Central Acropolis is in the distance.

altars. There are a great number of these monuments at Tikal and some are beautifully carved. Some are uncarved or in very poor condition. The Maya sculptors at Tikal did not reach the great florescence in monumental sculpture that is so evident at Copán. The earliest monument (Stela 29) excavated so far at Tikal has glyphs with the date A.D. 292.

At the base of the stairway to the Temple of the Inscriptions is one of the finest carved stela (Stela 21) at Tikal. The glyphs and the superb rendering of the foot on the standing dignitary serve to illustrate the Classic Maya ideal of beauty. This monument was found broken, with pieces scattered as far as a half-mile away. The stela can now be admired in its partially restored condition. Other important stelae that reflect the artistry of the Tikal craftsmen are Stela 22, with a date of A.D. 771, in Complex Q, and Stela 16, dated A.D. 711, in Complex N.

Occasionally there is archaeological evidence of human sacrifice among the Mayas. This is well illustrated in the temple murals at Bonampak, in the burial chamber under the Temple of the Inscriptions at Palenque, and also in a burial at Tikal. One burial (Burial 10) in the North Acropolis at Tikal contained a priest and, along with him, nine retainers who were killed for the occasion. Another evidence of human sacrifice is found on an altar at the foot of Temple III. Carved on the side of the altar is a tripod bowl that contains a human head. Near Temple IV at Complex N another monument (Altar 5) is carved with the figures of two priests standing behind an altar on which is placed a cranium and thigh bones. Other altars show carvings of bound prisoners who conceivably could be persons who would be sacrificed at the time the monument was dedicated.

In at least two instances howler and spider monkeys are represented on a stela (Stela 1 in the Tikal Museum)

Stela 16 is of particular interest because of the intricate detail of the dress of this important member of Maya society. The tombstone-shaped stela is not unusual at Tikal and is associated with Late Classic sculpture.

Although little remains of Stela 21, badly damaged during Late Classic times, the execution of the glyphs and the foot of this Maya nobleman attest to the sculptor's skill. The stela is located near the Temple of the Inscriptions.

and on an altar (on the platform of the North Acropolis).
Monkeys, common in this area, have also been subjects for
artistic expression throughout Mesoamerica. During Late
Classic times they were a favorite subject on Mayan pottery.
Monkeys were associated with promiscuity in Mayan myths
and are believed to have been used sometimes as a symbol
of fertility.

Many monuments at Tikal were deliberately destroyed
by being broken or defaced by their own people. This seemed
to be a common practice in several Mayan ceremonial centers during Classic times. Such destruction might have sym-
bolized a type of sacrifice to the gods. Another possible reason for destroying or defacing monuments could be to "kill"
the power of the priest or ruler depicted on the monument.
This practice may have been carried out at the time of the
ascendency of a new ruler. It is fortunate that this practice
was not in vogue at Copán, the fairest of all Mayan cities for
heroic sculpture.

Temple I rises 170 feet from the East Plaza platform to
the top of the roof comb. Since the area surrounding the
structure is completely cleared to the ground level, Temple I
is the most impressive of the pyramids. The single stairway,
sweeping from the plaza to the building platform, without
balustrades, is breath-taking. The view from the top of Temple I is unparalleled in the Petén. On the opposite side of
the Great Plaza is Temple II. In the distant jungle can be
seen the roof combs of Temples III, IV, and V. Temple IV,
the tallest in the Americas, is the one usually climbed by
visitors. There is only a dirt trail to give one a foothold while
attempting this extremely steep climb. Pyramidal bases for
these temples are quite similar. Stepped terraces with apron
moldings are the customary tectonic motif for the pyramids.
There is variation in the number of terraces and the treat-

The Great Plaza at Tikal. The North Acropolis is located on the right, and Temple II is at the end of the plaza. Temples III and IV can be seen on the horizon.

Temple II is also known as the Temple of the Masks. The temple at the top has three rooms similar in structure to Temple I. One of the original carved beams to the central lintel is preserved in The American Museum of Natural History in New York.

ment of corners of the pyramids. A single stairway was used to reach the summit of the pyramid. Temples crowning the pyramids have from one to three small vaulted rooms. In most buildings graffiti can be seen that date from Late Classic to Postclassic times. On the south side of Temple I is one of the smallest of all Mayan ball courts, built during the Late

Classic Period. Other ball courts are known at Tikal, the most unusual being a triple court.

Of the dozens of burials excavated at Tikal, of both ordinary and high-born persons, one of the most sumptuous graves (Burial 116) of an illustrious member of the opulent elite of Tikal was discovered at the base of Temple I. This personage, who died in Late Classic times, was buried with his ceremonial clothing, jewelry, and dozens of the most prized artifacts including pottery vessels and bone objects carved with glyph inscriptions and ceremonial scenes. The size of the graduated jade beads for his necklace, the jade bracelets, and other adornments total 180 pieces of carved jade weighing sixteen and one-half pounds. Most of these great treasures are now on exhibit at the Tikal Museum. Also at the museum is the second largest of all carved jades known to date, a lying, or sleeping, jaguar weighing three and one-half pounds, found in Burial 196 not far from Pyramid II. Another treasure in the museum is the four identical stuccoed wooden figures that depict the Maya rain god. The thin plaster is a pale blue. These sculptures were found with other artifacts in Burial 195.

Just beyond Temple II a dirt road leads to Temple III. Although a great portion of the temple on top of the pyramid is restored, the pyramid rises into a luxuriant tropical forest that completely encases it. The climb to the top of the pyramid is no more difficult than that of Temple IV, the one usually climbed by the visitor. Not only is the view superb from the top, but the reward of the climb is in seeing the carved lintel in the two-roomed temple. This wooden lintel and two beams of another in Temple I are the only remaining original carved lintels at Tikal. All others were crated off to museums in Basel, London, and New York many years ago. Lintels were carved of sapodilla wood, a very hard, durable wood that proved to be fairly resistant to insects. Although the lintel in Temple III is badly worm-eaten, the design can still be discerned. Covering an area of approximately fourteen square feet, the lintel is the largest of all at Tikal. Carved in bas-relief, the central personage stands in front of a throne, with two accompanying figures on either side. Glyph panels flank these latter figures. The important person portrayed in the central panel is immense, dressed in jaguar skins, wearing a headdress of a jaguar with quetzel feathers, and with adornments of jade pieces and shells. Because of the importance of the ceremonial dress on the central figure of the lintel, the temple is known as the Temple of the Jaguar Priest. Temple III rises to a height of 178 feet, considerably higher than Temples I or II.

The Central Acropolis, adjacent to the south side of the Great Plaza, contains over four acres of palace structures that ramble around six courtyards. This acropolis offered ideal residences for the Tikal aristocracy. The many courtyards gave privacy for individual families. All the buildings had a great number of rooms with vaulted chambers. The Central Acropolis was occupied from Preclassic times. Most of it still lies buried fifty feet below ground level, as excavations here have not been extensive. Consequently, the visible buildings range from Early through Late Classic times. The few Early Classic buildings can be distinguished by the size of the cut stone. Early Classic stones used for construction were somewhat smaller than those used for Late Classic structures. This change in the size of the cut stones can be seen on Structure 46, where the central building is of Early Classic date and the two side wings were added during Late Classic times.

In total, the Central Acropolis has forty-two buildings and hundreds of vaulted rooms. Most buildings face on

In Burial 195 at Tikal were found four identical stuccoed wooden figures of the Maya rain god. They are now in the Tikal Museum. The figures are sixteen inches high and date about A.D. 600.

Temple III looms one hundred and eighty feet above the Petén forest floor; it is known also as the Temple of the Jaguar Priest. The temple has two rooms, and between them is preserved the best carved lintel now at Tikal. Construction here was started a little over a hundred years after Temples I and II were built.

courtyards one story high, although a few buildings have more than one story. One of the more impressive buildings is the "Maler Palace" seen at the south end of Court 2, the largest court on the west side of the acropolis. This two-storied Late Classic structure was decorated with a frieze that encircled the building, but there is little indication of its remains today. Many of the buildings here have the original wooden lintels and cross beams used in the vault. Rooms on the back of the Maler Palace face the huge reservoir which supplied the water for this part of the ceremonial center. As seen today, it is a deep ravine filled with jungle growth. Occasionally a beautiful, blue, fragile motmot bird will be seen flying over the lush, tropical foliage.

The terrain on which the Central Acropolis is built is far from level. Consequently, the buildings and courtyards are on different levels, united by a maze of passages both inside and outside the palace structures. During the full moon, this area becomes a splendid viewing platform from which to survey the Great Plaza. On such a night Tikal is transformed into a mystic city glowing in the silvery blue light of the tropical moon.

Adjoining the east end of the Central Acropolis are three buildings that show a decided influence from Teotihuacán, the great Classic civilization of Mexico. One of these buildings has been excavated and is partially restored. Mexican influence in architecture and trade items, such as pottery, is noted in the Maya area at Tikal as well as at Kaminaljuyú in the Guatemala highlands. At this latter site, it is conceivable that the Teotihuacanos controlled the area for a short time. Because of the lack of fortifications at Maya cities during the Classic Period, it would seem the Mayans were not an aggressive, warlike people. Well-established trade routes made possible a great interchange of

The Central Acropolis at Tikal extends over an area of four acres on the south side of the Great Plaza. Only a part of this area has

been excavated and restored. The area is believed to have been
a residence for the ruling families or the priests.

luxury items from one cultural area to another. Transmigration of culture was an on-going process in Mesoamerica from earliest Olmec times through the Middle Preclassic Period (900–500 B.C.) until the Spanish conquest.

Four major causeways link together the various parts of the city of Tikal. Besides these, there are innumerable jungle trails uniting smaller plazas and complexes. After a few days at Tikal, there is time to see some of the more remote areas of the city. Complex P is especially interesting because of the carving on Stela 20 and the companion Altar 8. Along the Maudslay Causeway is the limestone quarry used for the restoration of Tikal. An early morning walk along the Méndez Causeway leads to the Temple of the Inscriptions, first discovered by Antonio Ortiz. The light at that hour makes the hieroglyphs on the roof comb and the cornice of the building clearer to see.

There are seven twin-pyramid complexes at Tikal. This unique type of architectural development evolved in the latter part of the Late Classic Period. There is evidence of this type of complex at Yaxhá, a ceremonial center southeast of Tikal. A twin-pyramid complex is constructed on an elevated plaza covering an area of five acres. The complexes are all similar. Two pyramids are placed on the outer edges of the plaza on an east-west axis. In front of the east pyramid is a group of plain stelae that might have been painted red at one time. To the south side of the plaza a nine-door structure faces into the court. The north side of the plaza has a walled enclosure with a vaulted arch for an entrance. In the center of the enclosure is a beautifully carved stela and altar. It is possible this enclosure may have had a thatch roof at one time. These unusual complexes must have served some new religious or ceremonial development. Best known of these is Complex Q, because of the extensive restoration here. The rest of the complexes are not restored. However, some of the areas are cleared so that the visitor can see the stela and altar associated with each of the complexes. Even though excavation has continued here for over ten years, most of Tikal is still buried under the jungle floor. That part that is restored is enough to suggest the grandeur of a great city.

It is quite possible that the ceremonial center of Tikal served as a capital for the people living in the surrounding countryside as far away as twenty to thirty miles from its center. It was here that the aristocracy directed the activities of the domain. The rank of the ruling family and possibly of priestly families was hereditary. Maya society was stratified, apparently with little mobility from one class to another. Paintings on pottery during Late Classic times give some indication of the relative status of various groups of people. A class of merchants, tradesmen, and craftsmen was more closely tied into the activities of the ceremonial center than farmers living farther from the capital. However, after the farming season was over, these peasants were expected to join that large body of humanity in the capital who physically built and rebuilt the great ceremonial center—a public-works program that was to continue for over a thousand years.

The Maya pattern of settlement in communities has been established by investigating elevated platforms used as the foundations of all homes and other buildings at Tikal. Some of the houses were built of stone and mortar. However, most houses were constructed of wooden frames of mahogany or cedar, the walls of sticks covered with adobe, and the roofs of palm thatch. Platforms for the houses were plastered. Mayan houses today are very similar to those built over a period of a thousand years.

Most burials for ordinary people were under the plat-

Stela 20 and Altar 8 were at one time associated with one of seven twin-pyramid complexes at Tikal. Although badly eroded, the standing dignitary can clearly be seen holding a staff as he stands in front of a jaguar throne. The design on the altar is similar to

others at Tikal in which a bound prisoner lies on his stomach with his feet tied behind his back. The monument is dated A.D. 751.

forms of the houses. Types of burials varied. Sometimes the person was buried in an area along the side of his house. He might be placed on his side, on his back, or in a seated position with the knees tucked close to the chest. Cremation was common in some areas, especially in the northern lowland region of Yucatán. There was no particular pattern in Mayan burials. The graves of ordinary persons were simple, while the ruling class and upper middle class had more elaborate graves of stone.

During Classic times, the pattern of settlement in Maya communities was a dispersed one. Houses were built around compounds that may have housed large family units. These units were grouped into small villages of 100 to 150 persons. Villages were the nucleus of peasant activity such as marketing, religious affairs, and social life.

On the basis of available evidence, we can get some idea of the life style of the Mayas. Village activities could have been directed by subchiefs who were in communication with the major ceremonial center of Tikal. Land probably was communal, controlled by the subchiefs who directed the system of *milpa* farming. This agricultural practice consisted of clearing the forest of trees by cutting and burning, planting the seed, weeding, and harvesting. "Slash-and-burn" farming was necessary because of the lack of draft animals to till the soil with plows. A family would farm one area for a period of four to eight years, according to the richness of the soil, and then would seek a new forest area for cultivation. When the people were not working in the field, they were subject to call by the elite at the ceremonial centers to contribute their labor to the arduous task of constructing and rebuilding the ceremonial center.

Guatemalan archaeologists have continued working on the restoration of Tikal since the University of Pennsylvania

This high corbeled vault is typical of many of the vaulted passages at Tikal. The "spindle"-shaped vault beams are unusual. They are located in the rear room of the Five-Story Palace in the Central Acropolis.

Through the corbeled arch can be seen a stela and altar that are associated with the twin-pyramid complex. This innovative type of architectural complex was devised during the latter part of the Classic Period.

ceased work here. The area of the Plaza of the Seven Temples has been cleared and one structure has been restored. Restoration has also continued at the Bat Palace and at Group G.

The future years should see many more structures restored in this great ceremonial center.

A walk on any of the jungle trails surrounding Tikal can be a startling experience. Jaguars still lurk in the forest, iguanas rustle in the dry leaves, and an occasional snake may be seen slipping away into a wet ravine. Moving in a single line, an army of leaf-cutter ants journeys over miniature trails on the jungle floor. The forest is a haven for strange-sounding insects, exotic birds, and other creatures. Showers yellow flowers drop from the tall palo blanco trees. There is an occasional amapola tree, with brilliant orange blossoms, that can be seen on the distant horizon. Mahogany, chicle, and cedar are the dominant trees in the forest. These are often covered with a countless variety of tropical vines and strangling figs. The scent of the allspice bush permeates the air when the leaves are crushed under foot. Orchids, ferns, bromeliads, and other epiphytes hang from the damp limbs of trees. This is the forest of Petén that the Mayas conquered and cultivated and in which they built their great city with its many pyramids thrusting toward the sky.

IV   The Motagua River Basin
Copán

(Wonderful trip)

A country road winds from the village of San José de Copán down to a fertile valley, over a stream used by the townfolk to wash their clothes during the cool hours of the morning, through the tobacco fields, and past the small airstrip adjacent to the ruins of the archaeological zone. The approach to the zone is through a thicket of trees where many old mounds are seen, still to be uncovered by the archaeologists. A pathway through the woods leads to the Great Plaza. The first view of the ruins is breath-taking as you gaze over the acres of courts and plazas surrounded by buildings and studded with heroic sculptured monuments. Ceremonial centers such as this one were the focal point for Mayan society.

Here is a ceremonial center unlike any other. At Copán one does not see great palaces with roof combs or intricate façades. Nor does he see high pyramids, conspicuous at other Mayan sites. Instead, the regional difference in sculpture and architecture is immediately apparent. The Copán Mayas created a ceremonial center that is unparalleled in terms of architectural beauty. There is restraint in the height of the buildings. Emphasis is on horizontal planes broken by monumental sculptures, a plan that establishes a sense of human scale and acts as a unifying force to the plaza. Around the Great Plaza bands of stairways covering several acres and encircling it on three sides create a quiet, sustaining dignity. The architects who planned Copán wanted it to be distinctive, unlike any other Mayan city. The approach to this cere-

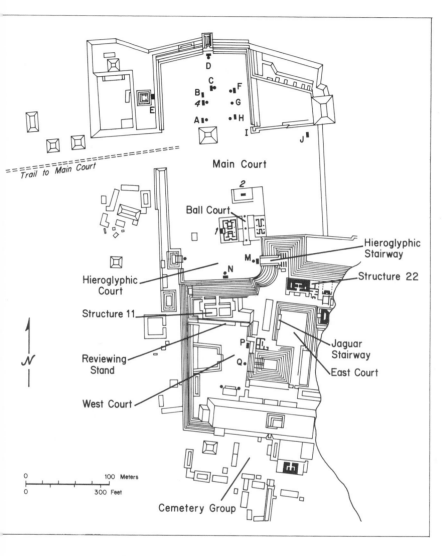

Main Court

D

C
B   F
4   G
A   H
  I
      J

Trail to Main Court

2

Ball Court

1

Hieroglyphic
Stairway

Hieroglyphic
Court

M

N

Structure 22

Structure 11

Jaguar
Stairway

Reviewing
Stand

P

Q

East Court

West Court

N

0   100 Meters
0   300 Feet

Cemetery Group

Copán
(after Morley)

75

monial center was designed to be an impressive one. The expansive plaza, with its many flamboyant stelae and "altars"; the ball court, a Mayan classic with its associated low buildings; the Hieroglyphic Court, a spectacular amphitheater for pageants; and the great palacelike structures leading to the East and West Courts at the southern end of the Acropolis must have been overwhelming to the casual visitor.

To understand the artists and craftsmen working at this time, to grasp the regional differences of this area compared with other Mayan centers, and to appreciate just how the various sections of this ceremonial center functioned, we must examine each of the parts of the center to get a comprehensive view.

The Great Plaza is distinguished by the location of some of the most important stelae and altars here. Visually so generous in terms of open space, it was well suited for the majestic ceremonies that we can assume were an intrinsic part of the Mayan society. Murals at Uaxactún and Bonampak, as well as pottery depicting ceremonial scenes, give some indication of ceremonial life. Elaborate ceremonies must have been required to appease the gods at crucial times in the life of the Mayas. The planting and harvesting season certainly required ceremonies. Great pomp and pageantry were essential at the time when rule was transferred from father to son. The appointment of officials to high posts in the Maya hierarchy would demand official ceremonies. There were also ceremonies associated with death, childbirth, and marriage. For many of these occasions the populace might be invited to participate. The ceremonies in connection with the great Maya sport, the ball game, were especially noteworthy. Since the Mayas at Copán were great astronomers and astrologers, ceremonies were associated with the important events in the Maya calendar. It was at such important times as these that stelae, altars, and buildings were dedicated.

At one time the floor of the Great Plaza was plastered and painted. Today it is kept as a green lawn dotted with twelve stelae. Many more are scattered throughout the ruins; some are in the distant hills and along the roadside. There are more fine carved stelae at Copán than at any other Maya site. These stelae are vertical stone monuments approximately ten to twelve feet high on which are carved full-figure portraits of rulers or important persons of the time. "Ceremonial bars" held in their arms may have been their scepters of authority. The carving is in high relief to a degree that some of the figures are nearly in the round. Nowhere else were figures carved in this manner. The sides or backs of these stelae have hieroglyphs that record specific time sequences as well as a variety of other data, much of which has yet to be deciphered.

At Copán the stone used by the carvers was a greenish-colored andesite. Because of its fine texture and even grain, the stone is ideal for carving. The quarry for the stone is less than a mile away, just over a hill en route to the village. Using only stone, bone, or wood tools, the sculptors' achievements are remarkable. The only disadvantage of this particular stone is that it occasionally has very hard, flintlike concretions shaped like cannon balls that sometimes protrude from the stone. Where these concretions appeared, the craftsmen had to use their ingenuity to cope with this unexpected disaster. There were several solutions, all of which were used at one time or another. They could incorporate these hard nodules into the over-all design; allow them to protrude and interrupt the design; cut them out, leaving hollows; or grind them down. This last arduous task was very time-consuming and difficult, since tools were of stone.

77

Detail of the head of Stela C. The original red paint, commonly used on stelae throughout the Maya area, can still be seen. Preservation of the color was due to the stela falling on its face many centuries ago, thus protecting it from the weather.

The color and texture of aged stone can be beautiful. Andesite is especially appealing, as the many centuries of weathering has bleached out some of the coloring where exposure to the sun has been constant. Blue-gray lichens and

The east face of Stela C is that of a more youthful man than the one on the west side. In the distance is Stela B. Stela C is dated A.D. 782.

Stela A, dated A.D. 731, is located in the Great Plaza near Mound 4. The face on this stela is one of the more sensitive ones carved at Copán. All the faces on stelae here are obviously portraits of people, probably rulers or members of the top echelon of Maya society.

This noble portrait of a ruler on Stela B shows a goatee, a popular fashion of the time. Goatees are also noted at the nearby site of Quiriguá. The diadem that acts as a crown to the headdress may have been made of shell.

yellow-to-orange algae also add coloring to some of the stones. During the time of Maya rule, the plazas and courts, the sculptures, and the buildings were plastered and painted in a variety of colors, red and blue being dominant. Traces of red can still be seen on some of the stelae. In the Great Plaza, Stela C is especially conspicuous with the weathered blotches of red paint. This particular stone shaft fell to the ground many centuries ago, preserving the color to this time. When Copán was reconstructed by the Carnegie Institution in 1934, Stela C was placed in its original upright position. This monument is unique in that it is the only one in the Great Plaza with two full standing figures, one facing the east and the other facing the west.

Of the many dignitaries carved on the stelae, a few of them have especially handsome, sensitive faces, attesting to the individual sculptor's skill and creative imagination. Of particular note are the face on the west side of Stela C, a most imposing man with a complete beard; the very Oriental-looking person of Stela B in a Mandarin-like headdress; and Stela A with a face as sensuous as any great master could carve. The important aristocrats on these monuments are clothed in the most resplendent garments, decorated with precious jade pieces and brilliant feathers of rare and exotic birds. Their regal headdresses are enhanced by the addition of elaborate masklike forms and zoomorphic creatures having special symbolic significance in terms of religion and social status. Much regalia on the headdresses may have been restricted to specific high-ranking persons in the populace. Zoomorphic forms were associated with certain priests or deities. On some of the stelae, what probably represented iridescent blue-green quetzal feathers, decorated with jade buttons and tassels, are extended from the headdress of the personage to his feet. Most of these dignitaries are laden

The back and sides of Stela A are carved in beautifully executed glyphs. Stelae at Copán rest over small cruciform chambers that at one time contained caches. The chamber for Stela A has purposely been left exposed so that visitors may study its construction.

Detail of a glyph on Stela A shows the encrustation of lichens and algae accumulated over the years. The affixes to the glyph are readily noticeable.

with anklets, bracelets, ear plugs, and pendants of jade. The usual dress was a breechclout, but in one instance a man wears a jaguar skirt. Shoes are of a variety of styles of sandals, some having high backs. The portrait-type faces on these monuments are in marked contrast to the highly stylized

Palenque faces having the swept-back foreheads and chins, the dominant curved nose extending onto the forehead, and other features that characterize the Usumacinta and Chiapas regions. Seemingly the Copán artists were not influenced by the more northerly Mayan cultures to any great degree.

Among the many impressive monuments in the Great Plaza, some are especially worthy of mention. The glyphs on the back of Stela A are as fine a carving as one may see at Copán. The glyph forms of this monument are made up of animal figures, human heads, and many abstract symbols. Another important monument, Stela H, has created a difference of opinion among archaeologists. Declared a woman and possibly a woman ruler by many, because of a skirt-type dress worn, the sex of this statue recently has been questioned by the noted scholar, Tatiana Proskouriakoff. She sees no reason to suggest that this is a woman, as the dress is characteristically that of a Mayan man, even though it is a skirt-type dress. The figure on Stela H wears a jaguar-skin skirt, and over this is worn an outer apron of jade beads. This same type of dress can be seen worn on male figures at Palenque on the stuccoed pillars supporting the façade to the Temple of the Inscriptions and the Palace.

Stela D, at the very north end of the plaza, has particular significance because of the full-figure glyphs carved on the back of the monument. Full-figure glyphs are a variant for numerals, but were seldom used. Three systems were employed by the Mayas for documenting numerals. "Dots and dashes" was one method to represent numbers from one to ten; "human head" (variants of these same numerals) was another; and the "full-figure" glyph variant is the third method. The full-figure glyph variant is no more than an extension of the head variant. Here at Copán the full-figure glyph can also be seen on the facing of the top step of the

Stela D overlooks the Great Plaza at Copán. This plaza was at one time plastered and painted. The hieroglyphic inscription on the back of Stela D has utilized full-figure glyphs. The stela is dated A.D. 736.

Stela H (left) depicts a male ruler in full ceremonial dress. In this instance he is wearing a jaguar-skin skirt that has a jade or bone apron crisscrossed over the skin. This particular dress is also seen at Palenque. At one time this stela was thought to depict a woman.

87

Hieroglyphic Stairway, and on Altar 41, the double-headed zoomorphic altar in the west end of the Hieroglyphic Court. Other sites having full-figure glyphs are Quiriguá, Yaxchilán, and Palenque.

Stelae at Copán are placed over a small cruciform chamber. In one arm of these chambers have been found caches of miscellaneous objects such as obsidian blades, pottery, and other simple objects that were used as offerings. Cruciform chambers under stelae are found only at Copán.

In front of most stelae is one of several types of low, flat monuments that we have called "altars." They may be round, square, or irregular in shape. As yet we do not know in what way the Mayas used the altars. Their shape seems to be of no particular help. In fact, some of these may have been altars, but there is no conclusive proof that they were. Most religions have altars that are associated with making offerings to the gods. Since the Mayan religion has a pantheon of gods, many types of offerings would be made, in different ways, and by the different social strata of their society. Even today the Mayas in remote regions of the countryside practice their older religion and leave offerings to their gods. These remote shrines and altars are located on mountainsides and in corn fields far from the touring public. Another purpose for the "altars" at Copán surely must have been as commemorative monuments serving a purpose similar to stelae.

The altar in front of Stela D is typical of many—a grotesque zoomorphic animal with two heads. Zoomorphic monuments may be a combination of several animals, such as serpents, turtles, jaguars, and frogs. Human features may be incorporated as well, such as human heads in the open jaws of serpents. In some of the altars it is no easy matter to tell exactly what animals the sculptors were trying to repre-

The use of two full standing rulers on one stela is unusual. This west face of Stela C is a portrait of a ruler who has a full beard, the only full-bearded figure at Copán. (However, there are faces on several stelae with goatees.) In front of the stela is a turtle altar.

sent. It would seem they had an attitude in regard to the animals on monuments that was more influenced by religious needs and social aspirations than by a wish to represent a given animal realistically. Quiriguá, just thirty miles from the Copán ceremonial center, is especially noted for large zoomorphic monuments.

Adjacent to Stela C is one of the most peculiar of altars at Copán. A shallow pond, circular in form, was made of stone and stuccoed. In this pond a very large sculptured turtle was placed. His head and legs were carved separately, giving him a feeling of mobility. Such sculptured forms as these and other zoomorphs added variety to the various sculptures in this Great Plaza.

Near Stela H is a group of three altars representing serpents. Two of the altars are identical—double-headed, feathered serpents with arched backs. The third altar is also in the shape of a double-headed serpent, with the serpent's jaws holding human heads. On the south side of this altar is carved the date in glyphs corresponding to A.D. 800[1]—the last dated monument to be carved at Copán. Shortly after this time Copán was abandoned. Tropical growth encroached upon the ruins until the nineteenth century, when John L. Stephens, the American explorer-adventurer, discovered the site.

There is a tendency for American Indians to be stereotyped as beardless. This is not wholly true, inasmuch as many Indians can and do grow beards. Beards must have been fashionable during the Classic Period at Copán, as figures on both Stelae B and D have goatees; on Stela C, a full beard; and on Stela F a mustache. Since the faces from several other stelae are missing, there may have been others with beards, too. Well over a thousand years before this time, the Olmecs in Veracruz carved monuments on which bearded persons are represented.

---

[1] All dates given are according to the Goodman–Martínez–Thompson correlation.

The Great Plaza at Copán is studded with beautifully carved stelae and altars. In the foreground is Altar G, the latest dated monument at Copán, A.D. 800. The unusual shape of the altar is that of a double-headed serpent in which human heads emerge from the serpent's jaws.

The eighth century is known as the Golden Age of the Mayas at Copán. Most of the sculpture and architecture at the site today is of that period. However, the preceding century was a vigorous one and not to be underestimated in

91

terms of productivity and artistic ability. From this earlier period there are two stelae in the Great Plaza, one in the West Court, and others scattered farther from the main site. In style these earlier figures have a decided somberness and stiffness. The sculptors had not freed their figures and costumes from the massive block of stone. The relief carving is not as deep, the feet face outward parallel to the front of the figures, and the carving has a slightly archaic feeling. During the next one hundred years stelae gradually changed. The feet turned farther forward as each decade passed until they reached a forty-five degree angle. Clothing became more ornate and the arms and legs of the figure more realistic. In Stela 4 the legs are carved in the round to a degree that they are nearly freed from the monument. Garments, along with methods of carving them, became more complicated, creating a baroque style that at times was ponderous. In the evolving style of the stelae we are aware of the cultural flowering of a people who knew their craft, worked within the framework of their tradition, and respected the experience of four centuries of previous sculptural achievements.

Stela N at the base of the Great Stairway to Temple 11 has the only filigree stone carving at Copán. The sculptor has carved an elaborate headdress nearly as large as the figure itself. This spectacular sculpture is complemented by the plain, expansive, imposing stairway. The pedestal on which Stela N is erected is the only one at Copán with hieroglyphic inscriptions.

The degree to which Copán influenced other cultural centers in Honduras, Guatemala, and countries much farther south has yet to be defined. The nearby site of Quiriguá is a case in point. Quiriguá, like all the other Mayan cultural centers, created its own regional style. An exception to this is Stela H (A.D. 751). On this monument the artist arranged

The back of Stela F is unique in that it has a rope design entwining five blocks of glyphs. Feathers arranged with buttons, a part of the dress of the ruler on the opposite side of the stela, sweep around the back of the monument, creating a pleasant pattern. The glyphs date the stela A.D. 721.

his hieroglyphs in a basket-weave pattern. There is only one other stela similar to it and that is Stela J at Copán, carved exactly forty-four years earlier. Quiriguá is not a great center, but it is an interesting one. From all indications, the area was not heavily populated, and the ceremonial center is small with few large structures. However, its craftsmen were highly skilled in carving. It seems quite possible that Quiriguá may have been controlled or dominated by Copán. Craftsmen from Copán may have been employed at Quiriguá to carve some of the monuments.

Next to the Great Plaza at Copán is the area intended for the most famous of all sports in Mesoamerica, the ball game. The Copán Ball Court is considered a classic in proportions, even though quite small. The court is in the shape of a capital "I," with buildings on either side. These could have served one of several purposes. Their function may have been as dressing rooms for the players, or as a place for the players to don their ceremonial regalia that was a festive part of the ball game. One of the chambers in the buildings could have been used by the priests as a place to appease the gods. The third possible use would be as an area for visiting dignitaries to bide their time before the start of the game. On the side walls of the Ball Court are benches (playing walls) in which hieroglyphic inscriptions run down both centers from top to bottom. It would seem that the Copán Mayas were highly preoccupied with the importance of recording data on buildings, and the Ball Court was no exception.

Excavations reveal two additional ball courts under this one, the earliest dating from the second century. Immediately under the present court the stone markers were circular and carved in low relief to depict players of the ball game in

tela J was the first monument carved after the Great Plaza was ompleted in A.D. 702. The stela is dated A.D. 707. The basket-weave design for the pattern of the glyphs is unique at Copán. However, a similar-type stela was carved at Quiriguá in A.D. 751.

The Ball Court at Copán is considered one of the best-proportioned courts in the area. Six parrot heads are tenoned into the benches and may have served as markers.

action. These markers as well as other artifacts from Copán have been removed to the little museum in the village. The present three markers running down the middle of the court are square. Markers might have been used as methods for scoring in the game or to indicate boundaries. Our only source of information on how the game was played is the Spanish account of the Aztec game, an account recorded over six hundred years later than when Copán was active. The game was played by two teams with from three to nine players on a team. A hard rubber ball weighing from six to seven pounds was used. The object of the game was to keep the ball from hitting the floor of the court while the teams tried to score. Because of the rough and tumble character of the game, it was necessary to have the knees and elbows padded as well as the loins and waist. The ball could only be hit with the elbow, knee, or hip. From the nature of the courts, there must have been many ways of scoring and playing the game. Ways of playing the game saw many changes over the centuries. Needless to say, the Mayas must have participated in innumerable types of ball games. Most ceremonial centers had several ball courts. Only one court has been reconstructed at Copán.

Six tenoned parrot heads are sunk into the slanting benches of the side walls of the court. This same type of head also has been found at La Union, just a few miles southeast of Copán. This latter site, along with Quiriguá, may have been under the control of one of the Copán chiefs.

From the Ball Court, the importance of the Hieroglyphic Stairway leading to Temple 26 now becomes appar-

The Hieroglyphic Stairway has the longest single inscription found to date. Glyphs are carved on the facings of all the stairs, approximately twenty-five hundred glyphs in all. The stairway is broken by five heroic figures. One was removed to the Peabody Museum in Cambridge, Massachusetts.

ent. A delicately controlled and sophisticated style prevails as one's gaze moves to the top. The facings on the sixty-three steps are carved with twenty-five hundred glyphs, the longest Maya inscription known. At five intervals in the center of the stairs are splendid, heroic, six-foot-high figures seated on thrones. The most handsome of these was removed many years ago to the Peabody Museum in Cambridge, Massachusetts.

On either side of the stairway a balustrade runs to the top, carved with celestial bird and serpent motifs, worked in an abstract design that leaves some question as to their identity. The balustrades are in marked contrast to the realism of the heroic figures. Serpents are generously used on stairways throughout Mesoamerica. The sculptors of most of the important Classic cities as well as those of the Postclassic phase adapted the serpent to a variety of innovative art styles. The serpent was the most important animal for decorative detail. Its undulating body lent itself particularly well to designs that could be applied to many architectural details on a building. Aside from this, the serpent was important in Maya mythology and as a fertility deity.

The Hieroglyphic Stairway should help in supplying the key to decipherment of the Mayan system of writing in the years to come. When the archaeologists were reconstructing the stairway, they concluded that approximately half the glyphs were restored to their proper place, although only thirteen steps were *in situ* before reconstruction began. Since earthquakes and roots of trees had disassembled a major portion of the steps, the task of reconstructing was in many ways like putting together a jig-saw puzzle. Stela M, located at the base of the Hieroglyphic Stairway, records a solar eclipse, an astonishing scientific awareness for that time. The date of the stela is A.D. 756.

On the stairway of the Reviewing Stand in the West Court are two grotesque figures holding what may be torches. Serpents are twisted around their waists, make up necklaces, and wreathe through the mouths of these unusual figures.

Looking at the Ball Court with its associated buildings, the adjoining Hieroglyphic Court with the famous Hieroglyphic Stairway, and to the north the Great Stairway leading to Temple 11, we become aware of the conscious thinking of the Copán architects in achieving a relationship and unity between the various buildings, stairways, and sculptured forms.

At right angles to the Hieroglyphic Stairway is the Great Stairway to Temple 11. This stairway acts as a divider between the northern and southern parts of the Acropolis. To the south is the West Court, an enclosure of nearly an acre, which gives the intimate feeling of a much smaller court. Stela P and at least three altars dating from an earlier period must have been brought into this court from another area after it was constructed. The practice of using older monuments in this way was also apparent at Tikal. However, there were times in Tikal's history when the monuments were destroyed or defaced. At Copán this was never a practice.

The Reviewing Stand on the north side of the West Court is an imposing edifice having a fifty-foot-long stairway that leads to Temple 11. At the top of the stairs, on the extreme sides, are two large, kneeling "torchbearers" with snakes in their mouths and around their waists. Three enormous conch shells are placed between these grotesque figures. Behind these sculptural pieces the wall has ten large niches, two having connecting rooms. They may have been used for the placing of objects during festivals, ceremonies, or commemorative events. The height of this platform and stairway suggests its possible use as a staging area for the pageantry occurring in the West Court.

The West Court is noted for the sculptured figures on Altar Q at the base of Pyramid 16. Carved in A.D. 776, the altar is believed to be dedicated to the lunar cycle. The top of this altar is sculptured in blocks of hieroglyphs. On each of the four sides of the altar are seated figures, sixteen in all, seemingly dressed as though from regional districts. All are seated on cushions carved with glyphs. The figures are all

This large head is believed to have been a part of the cornice of Temple 11. Over life size, it is an unusual provincial carving suggesting some of the humor of the time.

In the West Court, Altar Q is located near the highest mound in Copán. The top of the altar is carved in glyphs. Around the sides are sixteen persons seated on cushions with glyphs. None of their

...headdresses are alike. The altar was dedicated in A.D. 776 and is believed to record a lunar cycle.

facing toward the west side of the altar where the two central personages face each other as if in a commemorative gesture. They hold emblems of authority in their hands. Between the two figures is the date A.D. 763. If this represents a meeting of scientists or a council of scholars, the purpose could have been to witness the accomplishments of the astronomers in discovering the lunar cycle.

Sculpture showing the human figure seated cross-legged is uncommon at Copán. Other than Altar Q, the only seated figures are on the back of Stela B and on the top of either side of Stela N. Seated figures are more commonly depicted at Piedras Negras, Yaxchilán, and Palenque. They also frequently occur on ceramics of the Late Classic Period (A.D. 600–900). The Bonampak murals are well illustrated with this particular pose. A seated figure very similar to those on Altar Q appears at a far northerly site, Xochicalco, near Cuernavaca. Instances of the influence of the Mayas on other cultures as far to the north as this, and as far to the south as the Nicoya Peninsula in Costa Rica, are not uncommon.

Walking toward the East Court, an opening through the trees reveals the Copán River in the valley far below. This river has been eating into the bank of the Acropolis for many centuries, and as a result a portion of the East Court fell to its destruction during the landslides. One of the first major tasks in reconstructing Copán was to divert the course of the river, thus avoiding further catastrophe—a project that took two years. Along this area of the river bank there are still many mounds waiting to be investigated.

Most Mayan ceremonial centers have characteristics in common. They have stepped pyramids crowned with temples that face onto a central quadrangular plaza; palaces and ceremonial buildings clustered around smaller courtyards; platforms with flanking stairways as approaches to the buildings;

*Heroic jaguar on the wall of the Jaguar Stairway in the East
Court. At one time disks of obsidian were inserted for the spots
of the jaguar. Because of the importance of Temple 22, the East
Court may well have been the most important court at Copán.*

and stelae and altars as commemorative monuments. Regional differences in regard to construction, stylistic evolu-
tion, and ways in which ceremonial centers functioned varied
considerably. For instance, palace-type buildings surround-

Little remains of Temple 22 except the walls and the beautiful portal door sculptured in high relief. The decoration around the door consists of a double-headed serpent that is arranged over the top and down the sides of the door where its heads rest on Atlantean figures kneeling on skulls. This magnificent temple was dedicated to the planet Venus.

Stela 6 is on the side of the road from the village of Copán to the archaeological zone. It was dedicated in A.D. 682, just a few years before the completion of the Great Plaza at Copán. A number of stelae are located outside of the main archaeological zone. This massive heroic figure shows the more static style of sculpture that had evolved by the end of the seventh century.

ing the courts at Tikal provide very few adjoining rooms suitable for residency. However, there are many platforms and flanking stairways, making them ideal to observe pageantry.

The most important court at Copán may have been the East Court. The architecture is distinguished by a harmony of proportion and a decorative detail that is not only quite impressive but imaginative. On the west side of the court is the Jaguar Stairway, a unique contribution to the architecture of Copán. Two mighty jaguars, as tall as a man, stand in a most dramatic pose on either end of this stairway. These animals were carved to receive inlays of obsidian for the spots on their body. In the center of the staircase is an equally creative sculpture—the great rectangular Venus mask. This too is carved in very high relief. Like the Reviewing Stand in the West Court, the Jaguar Stairway may also have been used for watching ceremonial activities associated with the court. At times architecture, such as exemplified here, provides us with some understanding of the patterns of human behavior in a country where humidity has destroyed most other types of documentary evidence.

Facing to the north of the East Court, another magnificent stairway leads to the most important temple building in Copán, Temple 22. Here is one of the finest carved doorways to be seen in the Maya world. A baroque decoration consisting of a carved, two-headed serpent borders the doorway. Each end of the serpent is held up by an Atlantean kneeling figure resting on a skull. In marked contrast to the portal door is the serenity of the plain façade of the temple.

Traces of the original color can still be seen on the interior walls. As many as twenty-five coatings of plaster have been detected on the exterior of the building. The Mayas plastered and repainted their buildings periodically—usually

Stela B at Copán is one of the many handsomely carved monuments that have made this ceremonial center famous. The stelae here depict the many Maya rulers of the Late Classic Period.

One of the most interesting of the sculptured monuments in the Great Plaza at Copán is a spherical "altar" encircled by an entwined-rope design.

In the East Court at Copán is a monumental sculpture believed to be dedicated to the planet Venus. In the center is a head that may represent the sun deity. Late Classic.

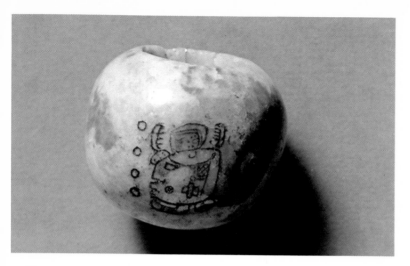

Toniná, burial site of an important Maya in Classic times, is the name given to a group of jades in The American Museum of Natural History. This beautiful large bead in white and green marbleized jade has the date A.D. 731. (Courtesy The American Museum of Natural History)

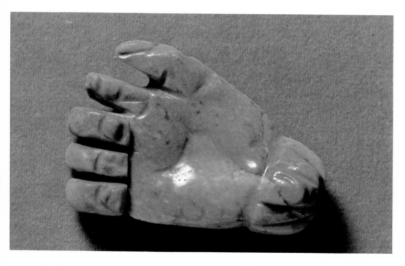

A jade talisman of a hand was part of the burial pieces found with the Toniná jades. (Courtesy The American Museum of Natural History)

Great Plaza and North Acropolis of Tikal from the Air. (Courtesy Mrs. Paul Williams)

Temple III emerges above the treetops at Tikal. The top of the temple is just 180 feet high.

Stucco portraits of the Mayas are highly stylized. This particular portrait (left) is of a young Maya elite, sensitively carved and then painted. Tabasco. Late Classic.

Portrait (right) of a Maya dignitary dressed in ceremonial clothing. This detail is part of a larger plaque located in the Tabasco Museum in Villahermosa.

In the East Court of the Palace at Palenque a narrative story is told in sculpture. This (left) is one of the nine figures assembled on both sides of the court stairway.

In the village of Sayaxché, Guatemala, is a handsome stela of a Maya personage dressed in ceremonial regalia (right). Late Classic.

Of all the ceremonial buildings at Palenque, the Temple of the Inscriptions is the most famous because of the rich treasure of jades found in the tomb under the pyramid.

In the lush rain forest adjacent to the Usumacinta River is the Maya ceremonial center of Yaxchilán. Structure 41 is one of the many hundreds of buildings here that have not been restored.

Much of the ceremonial center at Yaxchilán is buried under the jungle floor. The roof comb of Structure 5, shown here, is above ground. The rest of the building is intact below the surface.

The Palace of the Masks at Kabah is one of the very impressive palace-type buildings in the Puuc Hills of Yucatán. Late Classic.

Part of the Palace at Sayil in the Puuc Hills. The porticoed chambers on the second floor at one time opened on patios.

Entrance to an important courtyard at Labná is through the portal arch.

The Palace at Labná is one of the largest of its type in the Puuc Hills.

Sunrise on the façade of the House of the Magician, Uxmal.

Detail, showing a warrior, on the West Structure of the Nunnery Quadrangle at Uxmal.

On the edge of a cliff, overlooking the Caribbean Sea, is the site of Postclassic Tulúm.

The Observatory at Chichén Itzá, attributed to the Toltecs.

East Annex of the Nunnery at Chichén Itzá. An elaborate façade was created by the use of hundreds of mosaic stones. Late Classic Maya.

The Castillo at Chichén Itzá in the setting sun. (Courtesy Miss Alice Brody)

Throughout the ruins at Copán are sculptures located on the sides of walls and mounds, but they are not in situ. These two heads give the viewer some idea of the type of decoration the Mayas enjoyed on their buildings.

to coincide with the five-, ten-, or twenty-year cycle. These cycles were important commemorative times for erecting new buildings, stelae, and altars, and for rededicating monuments to the gods and ruling chiefs. This particular temple was dedicated to the planet Venus.

The whole platform adjoining Temple 22 is a glorious place from which to view the north end of the ceremonial center. In the late afternoon sun the courts are in deep shadows and the Hieroglyphic Stairway is sparkling in the warm glow of the filtered light. Large ceiba trees, deeply rooted in the ruins, drop their branches over the sides of the temple walls like ghosts from the past.

Returning to the village, on one of the grassy banks of the road are two large stelae facing the evening sun. These monuments are a part of a much earlier period in Copán than the Acropolis. The powerful-looking ruling chief carved on Stela 6 stands here as though to witness the conquests of future generations.

The ceremonial center of Copán influenced towns and villages along the Motagua and Ulua rivers that drain into the Caribbean, and the Pacific coastal areas from El Salvador down to Costa Rica. Many of the discoveries in astronomy and the refinements in the arts influenced other Mayan cultural areas to the north, and other cultures in the Mexican highlands. The contributions Mayan scientists and artists of Copán bequeathed to the rest of mankind is one that only a great civilization could have produced.

Quiriguá

The mist always seems to be present at Quiriguá. Even when the sun breaks through, it is only moments later that another shower sweeps the rain forest, spreading a rainbow across the moss-laden ruins. The Motagua River separates this rain forest area from the rich fertile valleys to the south where the ceremonial center of Copán is located. Flowing north

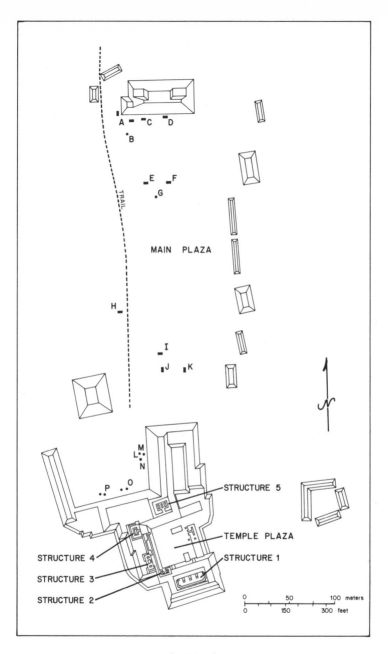

Quiriguá
(after Morley)

to the Caribbean Sea, the Motagua River parallels the northern boundary that separates Guatemala and Honduras. One of the sources for Mayan jade was the Motagua River bed. Here the boulders, smaller stones, and pebbles of jade were ground smooth by constant churning in the thrust of the river. It is quite possible the two-hundred-pound jade boulder found at Kaminaljuyú near Guatemala City was from the Motagua River. However, other river beds, as well as the Guatemala highlands, yielded jade too.

For many years the ruins of Quiriguá, as well as thousands of acres of banana plantations in the surrounding country, were owned by the United Fruit Company. Most of this property is now owned or controlled by the Guatemala government. The large hospital that was once maintained by the United Fruit Company now lies in ruin. In past years many a weary traveler, desirous of seeing the Quiriguá site, was graciously housed here for the night. Unitil 1970 a two-mile hike along the railroad track from the small village of Quiriguá was the only approach to the ruins. Now a road has been cut through to the area so that it is accessible by car.

The ceremonial center of Quiriguá is not a large one. The whole visible site is not more than ten acres. When the United Fruit Company bought the area in 1909 for their plantations, they set aside thirty acres for the archaeological zone, leaving the magnificent virgin forest surrounding the site untouched. Since the rain forest has not been cut back sufficiently from the ruins, the constant dampness has meant that the monuments and buildings are covered with moss and lichens and the buildings are overgrown by the constantly encroaching jungle.

Quiriguá was unknown to the outside world until its discovery by Stephens and Catherwood in 1840. Shortly after this the English archaeologist, Alfred Maudslay, spent some time at the site, and as a result the world is greatly indebted to him for his superb, finely executed drawings of the stelae and zoomorphs. Excavations were carried out by Edgar L. Hewett and Sylvanus G. Morley in 1910, at which time some restoration of two buildings was begun. The ceremonial site of Quiriguá had been abandoned over a thousand years ago, and during the passage of time many trees had fallen, knocking down monuments and crushing buildings. In 1934 the United Fruit Company engaged E. H. Morris and Gustav Stromsvik to reconstruct broken monuments and re-erect several that had toppled over.

The approach to the archaeological ruins today is by a path through the jungle adjacent to the railroad track. The first glimpse of the ruins reveals the Great Plaza. This Great Plaza is the only cleared area at Quiriguá. Jungle paths lead to excavated foundations, covered by the tropical forest in other parts of the site. From the Great Plaza, the most that can be seen is the series of stately stelae and zoomorphic monuments which command attention from all who visit here. Large mounds, covering old ruins yet to be excavated, exist all around the Great Plaza, well hidden by the mantle of green vegetation that envelops them.

Even though Quiriguá is a very small ceremonial center, there are many unique features that mark its individuality and its provincialism. The craftsmen here created the tallest monolithic sculpture in the Maya world. They also created the largest of zoomorphic monuments. The style of these heroic monuments as well as of the many other sculptures here is in marked contrast to the flamboyant style at Copán.

It would be difficult to believe that Quiriguá could have been completely independent from Copán. The two centers are only thirty miles apart. They functioned at the same time, reaching a great artistic climax during the Late Classic Period (A.D. 600–900). Since Copán is considered the most important scientific and cultural center of the Maya world, it is probable that the ruling chiefs and religious leaders at Quiriguá were related to those at Copán. Copán has a much earlier history, being occupied from Preclassic times. Quiriguá came into being during Late Classic times, with the earliest known monument dated A.D. 692. David Kelley has analyzed the hieroglyphic writing at Quiriguá and Copán. He traces Quiriguá dynastic rule for five successive ruling families, covering a period of seventy-five years. Further study of the glyphs may give us a deeper insight into the nature of Maya society.

Quiriguá's history really begins at a site near the old United Fruit Company hospital, approximately two miles away. At this early location are two stelae and a single temple. At a second center not far from this one, another stela was erected. The third location became the final one, with greatly increased activity and artistic production. Monuments here date from A.D. 711 to 810.

Upon entering the archaeological zone, the five tallest stelae are immediately visible. Stelae A, C, and D are in a line running from east to west. Just beyond these are the two tallest, Stelae E and F. Subject matter of the stelae at Quiriguá is the same as at Copán. A standing dignitary dominates one or two sides of the monument and descriptive glyphs are arranged to fill most of the remaining space. In many ways the attitudes of the figures on the various monuments as well as their dress are quite similar. At Quiriguá there is not the variety of form or the third-dimensional quality found at Copán. Faces of the dignitaries on sculpture at Quiriguá lack the sensitive individual expression noted at Copán.

There are some pecularities that can be pointed out in

regard to the Quiriguá stelae. The proportion of most figures is dwarfed by tall headdresses. The ceremonial bar signifying the staff of office as used at Copán is replaced on most stelae at Quiriguá by the "manikin scepter." The scepter, held diagonally in the right hand, consists of a staff with the Long Nosed God on one end, and the head of a snake terminating the leg of the manikin at the other end.

Another fashion of the time was the use of beards. Starting with Stela F, A.D. 761, beards were carved on the figures of all monuments for the next twenty-five years. Beards were the fashion thirty years earlier on stelae at Copán. Stela F is considered by some scholars to have the most beautifully executed glyphs. The most complex and intricately carved glyphs are on Zoomorph B, the large frog-like sculpture seen as you enter the archaeological zone.

The tallest monument at Quiriguá, Stela E, weighs sixty-five tons and reaches a height of thirty-five feet. The shaft of the stela was originally sunk eight and one-half feet into the ground, set in a foundation of rough-shaped stones and red clay. When Stela E was reset in an upright position in 1934, the shaft was set in a concrete block. To quarry such a large monument and move it to the ceremonial center is a major engineering feat. The quarry for Quiriguá is approximately three miles away. Here a fine sandstone, close-grained, even-textured, and ideal for carving, is found. To quarry the stone, it was first undercut in the shape of a rectangular block, the length depending on the sculptor's design. At Quiriguá the natural cleavage planes of the rock were taken advantage of and skillfully used. Pressure brought to bear along the length of the undercut stone by the use of wedges and plankings would break the stone free. Stone quarried from the living rock is much softer than after it has been exposed. As the stone ages, it becomes harder. Not

only is this true of sandstone used at Quiriguá, but lime-stone used at most other Mayan sites has the same physical characteristic.

From the quarry, the rough-cut stone may have been moved to the ceremonial center with the aid of skids. In some instances log rollers also may have been employed. It is quite possible that a part of the general shaping of the sculpture was completed before erecting the monument. The next engineering task was the erection of the monument. This was probably accomplished by means of ramps, utiliz-ing the great hardwood trees nearby, and by the use of ropes and cables that may have operated on the principle of a pulley when operated in the Y of tree branches. Once the stone was erected, the artist commenced the carving *in situ* by the use of scaffolding.

Stelae at Quiriguá range from ten to thirty-five feet in height. The red sandstone color as well as the restricted de-sign of the figures emphasizes the somber, more ponderous quality of these monoliths. Because of the hardness of this sandstone, carving in very low relief delineates most of the detail of the costume. The only part of the figure carved deeply by the sculptor is that portion around the head, and this is carved in very deep relief, the face being nearly in the round. In some ways this style can be likened to the stelae at Piedras Negras. Another analogy with Piedras Negras is the erection of monuments at the end of five-year counts. Piedras Negras and Quiriguá were the only sites that con-sistently erected monuments on this time interval rather than the ten- or twenty-year interval more often used at other Classic Mayan sites.

The accompanying chart shows the correlation of Maya

tela E is the tallest monolithic sculpture in Mesoamerica. Carved of sandstone, the stela weighs sixty-five tons. The monu-ment was dedicated in A.D. 771.

119

and Christian dates recorded on monuments at Quiriguá. Monuments at Quiriguá and Piedras Negras were erected at the end of 5 year cycle. At most other ceremonial centers monuments were erected at either the ten or twenty year cycle.

Stela	H	9.16.0.0.0	2	Ahau	13 Zec	=	A.D.	751
"	J	9.16.5.0.0	8	"	8 Zotz	=	"	756
"	F	9.16.10.0.0	1	"	3 Zip	=	"	761
"	D	9.16.15.0.0	7	"	18 Pop	=	"	766
"	E	9.17.0.0.0	13	"	18 Cumhu	=	"	771
"	A	9.17.5.0.0	6	"	13 Kayab	=	"	775
"	C	9.17.5.0.0	6	"	13 Kayab	=	"	775
Zoo.	B	9.17.10.0.0	12	"	8 Pax	=	"	780
"	G	9.17.15.0.0	4	"	3 Muan	=	"	785
"	O	9.18.0.0.0	11	"	18 Mac	=	"	790
Altar	O	9.18.0.0.0	11	"	18 Mac	=	"	790
Zoo.	P	9.18.5.0.0	4	"	13 Ceh	=	"	795
Altar	P	9.18.5.0.0	4	"	13 Ceh	=	"	795
Stela	I	9.18.10.0.0	10	"	8 Zac	=	"	800
"	K	9.18.15.0.0	3	"	3 Yax	=	"	805
Temple	1	9.19.0.0.0	9	"	18 Mol	=	"	810

Quiriguá stelae dates showing the Maya date and the equivalent date adjusted to the Christian calendar.

The stelae at Quiriguá date from A.D. 746 to 810, all within Late Classic times. The first stela erected at the present site is Stela H, with the glyph date of A.D. 751. This is an important monument, as it shows so obviously the influences of Copán craftsmen. In both Stela J at Copán and Stela H at Quiriguá, a diagonally woven mat design is used as a pattern for the placement of glyphs. However, the Copán stela was carved just forty-four years earlier. At Quiriguá the cruciform chamber-type pedestal popular at Copán was not used. Instead, the butt of the stela was sunk into the ground and held in position by rough-cut stones and clay.

The arrangement of the glyphs, on both the altars and stelae, is carefully designed to fill the total space provided by the artist. The Maya obsession to completely carve every part of monuments and altars is fully realized in the many baroque patterns on monuments here. The glyphs on Stela D that represent the year A.D. 766 are "full-figure" glyphs. These have been noted before at Copán. At Quiriguá they can also be seen on Zoomorph P, better known as the "Great Turtle Altar," as well as on Zoomorphs B and O.

The origin of the stelae-altar complex is unknown. The earliest dated monument of this type was found at Tres Zapotes in Veracruz—Stela C, with a date of 31 B.C. Undated stelae and altars were created by the Olmecs as early as the Middle Preclassic times. Future excavations in the Maya area and along its perimeter may give us a better understanding as to how this monumental sculpture evolved.

After erecting the enormous stone shaft, Stela E at Quiriguá, the carving of tall monuments went into a decline, with two dwarflike stelae ending the next five-year cycle. From this time on, Zoomorphs and altars were the popular carved monuments. Their function remains the same as those at Copán—to commemorate the social, religious, and scientific happenings important in the lives of the elite and their society. The shape of the zoomorphs alone would suggest that they never could have been used as altars.

Most zoomorphs look like crouching monsters. Usually double-headed and of composite identity, they have the general shape of an animal such as the frog, turtle, or jaguar. Reality in depicting animals was not a concern of the Mayan artist creating a zoomorph. For the most part there is great difficulty in telling exactly what animals were used as models. Zoomorph B is certainly close to the shape of a frog, whereas Zoomorph G is that of a jaguar. In both monuments a human head is in the animal's mouth. Glyphs are incorporated as a part of the over-all design of the zoomorph.

A depression in the ground, along a trail to the south of the archaeological zone, envelops Zoomorphs O and P. Zoomorph O is poorly conceived aesthetically and is not well executed. The Great Turtle Altar, or Zoomorph P, is by far one of the most magnificent stones carved by the Mayas. In the shape of a boulder, the stone is completely decorated in fairly high relief with intricate designs that are interlaced with human and animal forms combined with glyph panels. Only a great artist could have created this masterful sculpture, which transcends provincial differences noted in Mayan sculpture. The important personage seated in the jaws of this turtle-jaguarlike animal may represent a priest or ruler. His dress is elaborate; the headdress is intricate and exquisite in design; and a manikin scepter is held in one hand while a shield covers the other. The Great Turtle Altar, over nine feet long and seven feet high, must have been designed to be viewed from above as well as from the sides. A large mask form covers the top. A similar mask is repeated on the back of the zoomorph. These forms as well as many other related and unrelated designs are united by abstract curvilinear patterns and glyphs. Maya symbolism reaches its ultimate complex-

Zoomorph P is considered one of the most magnificent carvings in the Americas. The great stone is covered with a mantle of moss and lichens because of the constant dampness. Under this mantle the stone is elaborately carved in a florescent baroque manner. The stone is dated A.D. 795. The drawing accompanying the photograph shows details (after Maudslay).

ity in this monument. For many years this sculpture has been covered with moss and lichens, the roots of the plants eating into the surface of the stone. A few citizens of Guatemala are now considering the possibility of clearing away more of the jungle in an effort to stop this plant erosion. Scholars and travelers are quite discouraged to arrive at such a distant, remote region and not be able to study the designs or photograph the details on the monuments.

Two slab-type altars nearly level with the ground were discovered next to Zoomorphs O and P in 1934 during excavations there. The designs of the altars are quite similar. Carved in low relief, the subject is a masked dancer in a dramatic attitude of the dance. The remainder of the space on the small altar is beautifully carved with glyphs. Since these altars have been covered by the jungle floor for so many centuries, both are in mint condition. The jungle has been both destructive and kind to the handsomely carved monuments at Quiriguá.

Just to the south of the Great Plaza, the major platform of Quiriguá is reached by a flanking stairway. At this level is a group of major architectural structures, little of which can be seen today because of jungle growth. Only two buildings were restored, and then only partially. Architecture at Quiriguá is confined to smaller structures, simple in tectonic form and decoration compared to the great buildings at most other major ceremonial centers of the same era. The largest building is Structure 1, which may have been used as a temple. The building has three doorways that lead to inner chambers. Architectural style is simple, but distinctive. The façade is divided by a medial molding of hieroglyphs. Below this the wall is plain. Above the medial molding the wall is decorated in a fluted pattern and painted. The top step of the stairway leading to the temple is decorated with glyphs much like the stairway in the West Court at Copán that leads to Temple 11. The other excavated structure at Quiriguá, located just below Structure 1, is a smaller building designated as Structure 2. Since it has only one chamber, it may have been used by the priest or a chief as a dwelling. Decoration on this building consists of mosaic heads at the corners and on the outer walls. Today the dense jungle has engulfed most of the architectural structures.

As the midday light penetrates the foliage of the mighty hardwood trees to the plaza floor, Quiriguá becomes a sheath of shimmering green. The trees must have been a decided asset to the Mayas. Here was wood in unending quantity for the cooking fires, construction of houses, traps for animals, ceremonial decoration for festivals, and countless uses later assigned to metal, unknown to the Mayas during Classic times. The only known metal objects at a Classic site were found at Copán in the cruciform chamber under Stela H; they were two crushed limbs of gold that were part of an offering. Analysis of the gold would indicate that the objects were imported from either Panama or Colombia.

Endowed with rich, fertile soil for agriculture in the area surrounding the ceremonial center, tropical forests on the distant horizon, and a wealth of technical skills passed down from one generation to another, the Mayas at Quiriguá created a social order in this rain forest that has had no equal since Classic times.

V   Lower Usumacinta River
Palenque

The swampy, palm-studded plains stretch from the Tabasco coast to the northern slope of the sierra of Chiapas. This is a country of pastureland when the season is dry enough, and one of flooded rivers and streams during the rainy season. One sees egrets and cranes hovering over the vast water areas that are already filled with ducks, grebes, and other waterfowl. The rains, heaviest in all Mexico, have produced an exuberant tropical-rain-forest environment between the Palenque ruins and the adjacent mountainous region. The valley's fertile land is just as rich for farming today as it must have been over one thousand years ago when Palenque had reached an apogee. The region abounds in natural resources, from the tropical forests to the grasslands and swamps. This environment was one the Mayas readily realized would be perfect for their ceremonial center.

Just a short distance away, the Usumacinta River was easily available for use, becoming one of the great "highways" for the Mayas. With no wheeled vehicles or draft animals, waterways were the easiest and cheapest means of transportation. The Usumacinta was especially important because trade produce could move easily along the Bay of Campeche and through the Usumacinta River system to the Petén. This important artery made possible communication from one ceremonial center to another. The ruling chiefs in their great canoes could attend festivals and important ceremonial events in other towns and cities. Architects and artists could exchange their views on techniques and styles being created in the various areas. From the Usumacinta and Pasión River system communications could be extended overland through the Petén to the Maya mountains. Here, the Belize River flows to the Caribbean. Farther south, overland routes from the Petén connected with the Motagua River and other river systems used for transportation by the Mayas. Because of this communication system there was a degree of unity within the Mayan civilization.

The elevation of the Palenque site gives it a commanding view of the great plains stretching to the distant horizon. Just five miles away is the little village of Santa Domingo Palenque—the closest town for the traveler to spend the night. The fern-covered mountains and wet forest that circle behind the ruins act as a shimmering green screen for the great palace, the temples, and the residences that dot the surrounding hillside. Natural hillocks were used as bases for some of the buildings, and when there were no such hillocks, pyramids were constructed, elevating the buildings high above the ground level. Some buildings were sheared against the mountainside, and artificial terraces and stairways were then constructed over this natural escarpment.

Hillside ceremonial centers, where buildings are constructed at different levels on the sloping terrain, were common along the lower Usumacinta River. As far as possible the buildings were oriented to the cardinal points, but in most instances uneven terrain dictated the direction of the building. Palenque, Yaxchilán, and Piedras Negras were the largest and most imposing ceremonial centers along the Usumacinta—each quite distinctive in its plan, in architectural style, and in sculpture. Although smaller ceremonial centers such as Quiriguá and Bonampak may have been under the suzerainty of larger centers such as Copán and Yaxchilán, for the most part the Mayan cities and their sur-

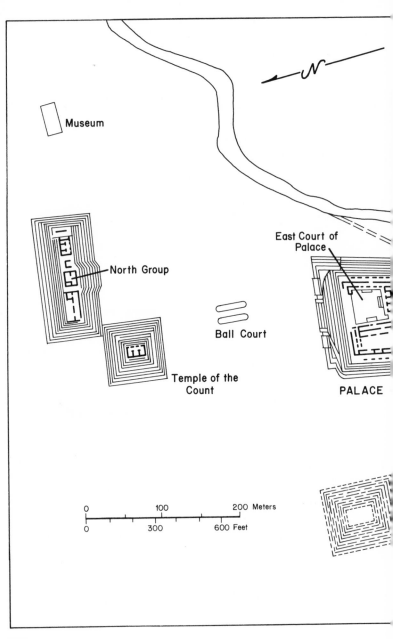

Museum

North Group

East Court of
Palace

Ball Court

Temple of the
Count

PALACE

0   100   200 Meters
0   300   600 Feet

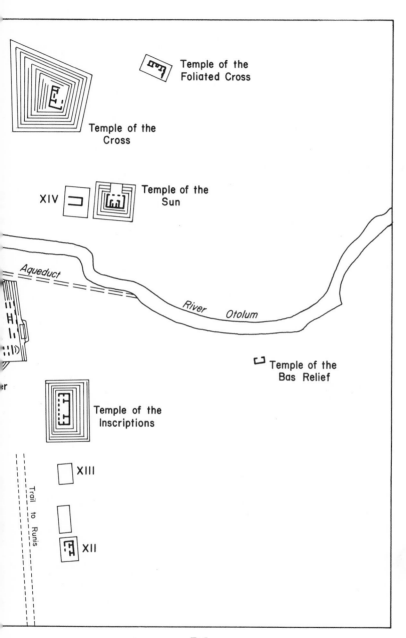

Temple of the
Foliated Cross

Temple of the
Cross

XIV

Temple of the
Sun

Aqueduct

River   Otolum

Temple of the
Bas Relief

Temple of the
Inscriptions

XIII

Trail to Ruins

XII

Palenque

Aerial view of Palenque. The large building in the lower right is the Palace. Surrounding the ceremonial center today is the rain

...rest, which covers hundreds of mounds, terraces, and platforms ...at were once part of the ceremonial center of Palenque.

The Palace at Palenque. This palace-type structure had ma[n]y additions and renovations over a period of several centuries. T[h]

...ur-storied tower dominates the area and is unique in Maya ...chitecture.

rounding territory were autonomous. These loosely knit city-states were unified to the degree that religion, science, the arts, and other cultural endeavors were concerns held in common. The Mayas brought their civilization to its high level not as a warlike conquering people such as the Aztecs and Toltecs, but by sharing common interests and working together toward common goals. The advancements in the fields of writing, astronomy, and mathematics could have been attained only through interaction and exchange between the great Mayan centers.

The ruins of Palenque have been known since the eighteenth century. During the nineteenth century many noted archaeologists as well as a host of distinguished travelers visited the ruins. The list includes such names as John L. Stephens and Alfred Maudslay, noted for their adventures throughout the Maya area; Frederick Waldeck, a classical artist who lived in one of the temples at Palenque for three years; Désiré Charnay; and Edward Thompson, who wrote articles on Palenque toward the end of the century. Shortly after this time Sylvanus G. Morley, Eduard G. Seler, and Franz Blom carried out archaeological reconnaissance at the site. Actual restoration was first under the direction of Miguel Angel Fernández and administered by the Mexican government. Later, Alberto Ruz Lhuillier continued the restoration here, and it was he who made the remarkable discovery of the tomb in the Temple of the Inscriptions.

Palenque is the most beautifully conceived of all Mayan cities. The architecture is inventive in design and well adapted to the humid climate. Stucco decoration on the buildings is the most delicate and sophisticated of any found in Mayan areas. The art is an expressive one portraying the life of the elite, highly disciplined and seemingly at peace with the outside world. There is no suggestion of violence,

penitential scenes, or sacrifices so often portrayed in the art
of Yaxchilán or Bonampak. The tranquillity that prevailed
at Palenque throughout Classic times helped produce its
brilliant culture, a highlight of Mayan civilization.

On approaching the archaeological zone one sees many
earthen mounds covered with dense undergrowth, indicating
the work yet to be done by the archaeologist. The total story
of the magnificent ruins here has yet to be revealed. However, the site as we see it today is awe inspiring. Usually a
light rain is blowing in over the mountains, creating a vapor
of green mist that gives an effect similar to a Sung Dynasty
painting. Against this soft, lush green color are the naked
white buildings, denuded of their brilliant color and stucco
decoration by the centuries of constant tropical rains. Unfortunately, stucco is the most perishable of all decorative
techniques in a rain forest.

The Palace, a complicated network of buildings, vaulted
galleries, patios, courtyards, porticoes, and subterranean
chambers, went through many alterations during its long
occupancy. This imposing structure covers approximately an
acre and is situated in a central area of the ceremonial center
so that the façades of all other buildings face toward it. Although most of the Palace buildings are only a single story
high, in the southwest corner is a tower four stories high.
This tower may have been used as an astronomical observatory or as an observation post to announce the arrival of
important dignitaries. The tower is unique among Maya
edifices. Beneath the southern end of the Palace structures
are subterranean quarters with many rooms, indicating an
earlier occupation here. The present Palace structures were
no doubt built over these subterranean rooms at a later time.

The west side of the Palace is flanked by a palatial stairway leading to a porticoed chamber. The piers between door-

This stucco decoration on a pier of the Palace depicts a narrative scene where a standing dignitary is attended by two seated figures at his sides. The person on the left is believed to be a woman—not often depicted in Maya sculpture.

The piers between the doorways of the porticoed chambers at Palenque are all beautifully decorated in stucco. Persons adorned in ceremonial dress may be important members of the ruling family. Some of their attitudes would suggest dancers. Palenque Palace.

Detail of a narrative scene on the piers of the Palace at Palenque. Although badly damaged by the weather, these stucco decorations are some of the most beautiful sculpture of its kind in the Maya world (above and right).

ways of this vaulted chamber are of particular interest. Each of the five existing rectangular piers is decorated in stucco relief. Many portions of the stucco are missing or weather-worn. And, of course, the color has washed away except for scanty traces on some figures. The piers depict full human figures of the noble class of people (some may be dancers), dressed in ceremonial or courtly clothing. Palenque sculptors were masters in decorating buildings with stucco, a material

The East Court of the Palace. Where a section of the mansard
roof has fallen, it is possible to see the corbeled trilobate open-
ings between the Palace walls. On either side of the stairway

to the court are sculptured panels depicting a narrative scene.
These panels may have been a later addition to the court.

On the right side of the stairs to the East Court of the Palace are five figures of persons sculptured in low relief. Instead of the usual formalistic Classic Maya style encountered at Palenque, this narrative scene is sculptured in a realistic provincial style.

made of fine, powdered lime mixed with water. In paste form it was applied as a decoration on walls and piers at Palenque. The medium seemed ideal for the Maya temperament. In these decorations are some of the most exquisite lines, delicate contours, and sensitive expressions found in any of the great sculpture of the world. These stuccos are creations of the imagination, indicative of artists with great talent and

This head detail shows the skillful rendering by the sculptor of a member of Maya society.

ability. There is an elegance in the modeling that contributes to a refinement in style which could only evolve over a period of time with no major interruptions from external or internal sources.

The Palace, like all buildings at Palenque, has a mansard-type roof which was completely stuccoed in bas-relief with delicately sculptured scenes representing rituals, ceremonies, deities, and other subjects in a highly conventionalized style. Buildings were given added height by the addition of extremely high roof combs. As we see them today, they are perforated. However, during Classic times these roof combs were covered with a carved-plaster embellishment and then painted. The roof combs are quite impressive against the leaf-green forest behind them. The technique of constructing these combs is clearly seen by climbing the stairway that circles the inside of the four-storied tower and then peering down on the roof.

Several architectural features of the Palace are unusual. One of these is the great trilobate arch that leads to the East Court. This same type of arch was used in the construction of niches in the interior corbeled rooms and passageways of the Palace. It is also noted in other temple structures as well. The shape of the arches is reminiscent of those in the Islamic world. The Mayas at Palenque indulged in the use of the curved line in architecture, thus creating a new form. Creative ingenuity of Homo sapiens can have many parallels in many regions in the world, and this arch is only one of many similar developments.

In the East Court of the Palace there are many panels and stair facings carved in especially fine low relief. From the style of the sculpture, and the alterations noted in the construction of the court, we can assume that many decorative and architectural changes were made here over the centuries. In contrast to the usual formalistic style of Palenque figures, there are nine life-size figures on either side of the steps of the court sculptured in an unparalleled naturalistic style. The two figures closest to the stairs have their heads turned up as though in respect to someone at the top. Six of the other figures could be priests or members of the ruling family who have been involved in some type of judgment in regard to the narrative scene depicted by the nine persons. The ninth person may be the one who received the judgment, as he is the only one in the nude, and he may have come to this disgrace by breaking the mores of the society. The expression on his face indicates great anxiety.

On the opposite side of this court are two additional life-size figures on the balustrade of the stairs. Similar figures are carved in stone on the balustrade of the top platform to the Temple of the Inscriptions.

Close examination of the East and West Courts of the Palace indicates that these carved panels on the lower portion of the platforms surrounding the courts were refaced during one of the many renovations. This may have been done to reinforce the substructure of the court as well as to enhance its beauty.

Located at intervals along the façade of the Palace, facing the Temple of the Cross, are stucco cartouches decorated with tropical leaves and flowers in a rococo style. At one time these panels framed stucco heads. Unfortunately, these have all disappeared with the arrival of greedy visitors, collectors, and looters.

Palenque is noted for a series of finely carved panels and tablets. The most important one, uncovered in the north end of the Palace by Alberto Ruz, is from the seventh century. The scene is of an offering, and the panel is especially important because of the 262 hieroglyphs. It is this panel that utilized "full-figure" glyphs for numerals. Full-figure glyphs were also used at Copán, Quiriguá, and Yaxchilán.

Throughout the Palace are indications of patterned designs painted on the plaster both on the external and internal walls. A steam bath, urinals fed by water ducts from running streams under the floor of the Palace, altars, throne benches, air vents, and other utilitarian innovations can be seen in various parts of the structures. The high vaulted ceilings here, as well as those in other buildings of this archaeological zone, was another clever invention of the architects to keep the rooms cool. By the use of double-vaulted ceilings, porticoes, and doorways, the rooms were

145

Temple of the Inscriptions, famed for its burial chamber, rises on a terraced platform that is backed against a steep hillside which encircles Palenque. It was here that Alberto Ruz discovered the stairway that led to the tomb, possibly of a priest buried here in the seventh century.

made light and airy, especially in comparison with the dark, small chambers in the temple buildings at Tikal in the Petén jungle. It would seem this palace was much more functional than those at other Maya cities. The dozens of rooms for the housing of such persons as the rulers, chiefs, priests, and lesser nobles would indicate a large populace at the cere-

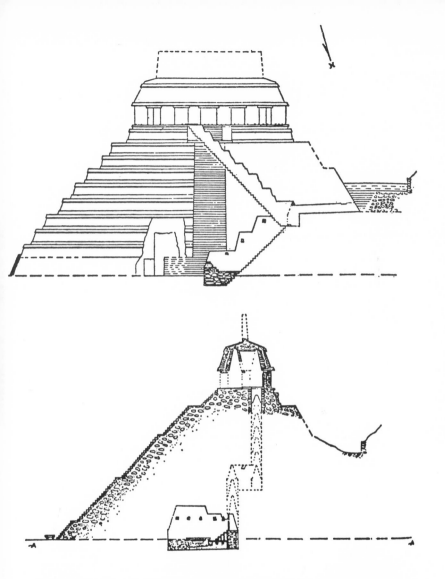

Temple of the Inscriptions, Palenque. Elevation and section to show the interior staircase leading from the rear room of the temple to the burial crypt. A light and ventilation shaft led from the stairway landing to the exterior of the pyramid. (After A. Ruz, from J. Eric S. Thompson, The Rise and Fall of Maya Civilization*)*

monial center. Large rooms with spacious open courts at the northern and eastern ends of the Palace were most likely those reserved for ruling chiefs. Smaller apartments and rooms at the southern end of the Palace could have been for visiting guests and persons of noble status. Other rooms could have been used to house the servants and to serve as utility rooms.

The Temple of the Inscriptions is one of the great monumental structures at Palenque. Its fame is due to the tireless energy of that remarkable archaeologist, Alberto Ruz Lhuillier. It was he who discovered the secret passage in 1948 and during the four following seasons excavated the stairway that leads to the magnificent royal tomb of Palenque.

Eight stepped terraces form the base of the pyramid that is crowned by the Temple of the Inscriptions. The terraces are banded by binding moldings, creating pleasant horizontal frames for each terrace. A single, narrow stairway, having no balustrade, leads to the top of the pyramid. The back of the pyramid is built partially into the side of a steep limestone hill. Behind the temple, a tropical forest frames the whole structure, giving it dimension. The mansardlike roof, once covered with beautiful stucco, had an ornate roof comb. Little of it is left today. Rising seventy-five feet above the plaza, this building is the highest at Palenque. With the roof comb, the temple was approximately another forty feet higher. The five doorways to the temple are separated by four piers decorated in stucco in the same style as those on the Palace. The subject on the four piers is similar and may be narrative in form. An important person holds a child in his arms. This may have been a young prince held by his father or some other lord of the Palenque realm. The decoration on one of these piers depicts a man of noble class wearing a dress made of jaguar skin, over which he wears an apron of jade beads. The jade-bead apron is identical to that carved on Stela H at Copán. The type of dress worn by these men is another reason to believe that the figure on Stela H at Copán, designated as a woman at an earlier time, may in fact be a man.

Entering between the piers of the Temple of the Inscriptions, one is in a large vaulted chamber with three panels containing one of the longest of Maya hieroglyphic inscriptions. Glyphs on the panels cover a chronology of some two hundred years. The panels were dedicated in A.D. 692.

One of the keys to discovering the secret stairway leading to the tomb was finding circular holes, plugged with stone inserts, located in a slab of the floor. These holes were used to lower the large stone slab into place when the Mayas closed the tomb. The descent down the tunnel-like stairway is accomplished with the aid of a flashlight. There is electricity, but power is available only for a short period of the day. Since the famed tomb is five feet below the level of the plaza, one descends on the dark, damp, slippery stairway to eighty feet below the temple floor. To peer into the tomb and see the sarcophagus is a thrilling moment in anyone's life. Even though the contents of the tomb have been moved to the Museum of Anthropology in Mexico City, the sarcophagus is still here, with its beautiful carving in low relief. The walls of the crypt are decorated in stucco reliefs representing Mayan deities. Those depicted here are believed to be the Nine Knights or Lords of the Underworld, who ruled the subterranean world. Comalcalco, a Maya site not too far north of Palenque, has a similar type of decoration in one of its structures.

The middle-aged noble (possibly a priest) buried here was covered with jade ornaments consisting of ear plugs, pendants, beads, rings for each finger of both hands, and a jade mask consisting of two hundred pieces of jade. In the tomb was another smaller mask of jade representing an older man, two beautiful jade figurines, and two life-size stucco heads. These two heads had been broken at the neck, indicating that they were removed from some other part of the ceremonial center and placed here when the crypt was closed. Both faces suggest the sensitivity of the artist who created the portraits. Pieces of jade were placed in each hand and in the mouth of the dead ruler. This custom is similar to an ancient Chinese ritual for the burial of the dead. Pottery pieces were also found; these most likely contained food and drink as offerings to the gods. Before the tomb was closed, the whole chamber was sprinkled with red, powdered cinnabar, much used for burials throughout Mesoamerica. The red color is symbolic of the east, the rising sun, and resurrection.

Outside the tomb wall the skeletons of several youths were found, left possibly to act as guardians for the tomb. When the Mayas had finished the burial, they filled the stairway that leads to the temple above with rubble. In designing the stairway the architects arranged for an air duct to run from the tomb up the side of the stairs to the temple floor. This duct can be seen along the side of the stairs today. This air passage could have acted as a means of communication from the crypt to the celestial world of the Mayan deities. Stone and clay tubes have been found in burials over a thousand years older at Tres Zapotes and Monte Albán. The tomb under the Temple of the Inscriptions is not the only one found at Palenque, but it had by far the most outstanding treasure here and is the only one of its kind to be found in the Americas.

Looking from the Palace to the east, one can see three

The three small temples in this area are noted for their beautifully carved panels in the inner sanctuaries. Hieroglyphs on the
back panel of this temple, Temple of the Sun, give a date corresponding to A.D. 642.

Rising from artificial platforms that once were plastered and
painted are the Temple of the Cross, Temple of the Foliated

Cross, and Temple of the Sun. These structures were all built during Late Classic times.

small temples quite similar in architectural design, all on artificial terraces having pyramidal bases. The most impressive of these is the Pyramid of the Sun. The other two, the Temple of the Cross and the Temple of the Foliated Cross, are smaller in size than the Temple of the Sun. They face onto a central plaza which may have been important for the festivities that took place in this part of the ceremonial center. All three buildings were highly ornamented in stucco decoration, including high roof combs, friezes on the mansardlike roofs, and piers between the temple doors. Of greatest importance in these temples are the superb panels in low relief carved for the wall at the rear of the inner vaulted sanctuary. The subject of the panels in all these temples is similar. Two priests or rulers, one larger in size than the other, flank a central symbolic motif of a cross, sun, or maize god. The panel in the Temple of the Cross was removed to the museum in Mexico City. Adjacent to the Temple of the Sun is the recently excavated Structure 14. This temple is of a design similar to the other three structures here, but restoration is only partial. One of our earliest portrayals of an Indian smoking a cigar is carved on a panel in the Temple of the Cross. J. Eric S. Thompson believes sapodilla leaves or allspice leaves were used to wrap the tobacco. Tobacco was also powdered and mixed with lime in much the same way that a mixture of pepper vines and lime is used by peoples of the South Seas. Lime activates the chemicals in tobacco and produces a stimulant. The tired, weary Indians found this refreshing after a hard day's work. Cocoa leaves also act as a stimulant when chewed. These can still be bought in the markets of Central America, Bolivia, and Peru.

Hieroglyphs are an integral part of the design of panels found in both the temples and the Palace. The dating of the temple panels suggest a span from A.D. 642 to 692. The Palace panels have later dates, corresponding to A.D. 720 and 783 according to the most accepted system of dating. Of these three structures, the Temple of the Sun has had the most restoration and is in fairly good condition. Neither of the pyramids to the Temple of the Cross or the Temple of the Foliated Cross has been restored. The front half of the Temple of the Foliated Cross collapsed long ago and tumbled down the embankment. From the platform of this temple, a superb view of the whole ceremonial center and the surrounding countryside is possible on a clear day.

During the rainy season hundreds of little streams swell into rivers and pour down from the limestone cliffs behind the ceremonial center into the Otolum River. Mayan engineers designed a system of bridges over this river to have access to the temples on the other side. In addition to the bridges, they built a vaulted aqueduct of stone, nine feet high, to direct the stream under the plaza floor. During the late spring and summer when the rains are not heavy, the Otolum River dwindles to a little stream. Not too many years ago, when travelers slept in hammocks in the village and there were no washing facilities, this stream was handy for a quick bath—quite refreshing after a hot day's work in the sun.

Between the Palace and what is referred to as the "Northern Group" is a small ball court that has not been reconstructed. The Northern Group consists of five buildings on platforms at different levels, flanked by stairs. Varying greatly in size, the buildings were probably temples serving different functions and constructed for different purposes.

To the west of the Northern Group is the Temple of the Count, so named because Frederick Waldeck used the building as a residence for three years during the early nineteenth century. This building has been more completely restored than other buildings in the Northern Group.

Just to the east of the Northern Group is a small museum housing some of the treasures found at Palenque. Here it is possible to carefully examine the panel of glyphs found in the Palace. The pottery, jade, and stucco decorations from various excavations are also displayed. Just outside the museum is a carved figure in the round, the only one here that has any resemblance to the type of stelae used commonly at many sites during Late Classic times.

Palenque was not a city of high pyramids or of great stelae. In fact, no prism-type stelae have been found. Nor was it a city that had a high production of pottery. Its history began in Preclassic times, with some indication of occupancy during the Early Classic Period (A.D. 300–600). Its flowering coincided with the Late Classic Period (A.D. 600–900). The decorations carved in stucco are highly individual. Designs of the wall panels and plaques are those of master craftsmen who possessed great technical facility and artistic ability. The refinement and subtlety of their aesthetic expression are highly expressive—unique to Palenque. The linear style here is in great contrast to the robust, rococo style used by the Copán artists. Both are very much a part of the great Mayan tradition in the arts: Copán, the outstanding center in the southern limits of the Maya world, and Palenque in the most northerly sector. Architecture in both these extreme geographical areas stresses the dominance of the horizontal line. This is accomplished by binder moldings that encircle terraces, cornices, doorways, and platforms. The moldings create shadows that emphasize the horizontal line and thus act as a unifying force for the entire architectural complex. There is a close tectonic relationship in the

A small oratory-type structure in the Northern Group at Palenque.

placement of the buildings at different levels and the terrain. The Mayan city planners always seemed to be conscious of the environment and the terrain in which they were to build. At Palenque in particular there is a harmony between the natural forces and the efforts of man.

Yaxchilán

Yaxchilán has hardly been touched in modern times. Today the ruins lie largely buried under earthen mounds that have been cleared of trees and scrub. A number of buildings rise above the mounds that cover the substructures. Over the doorways of these temples and palacelike buildings are the handsomely carved lintels that have made Yaxchilán one of the most outstanding of ceremonial centers for fine stone carving.

Yaxchilán is in the state of Chiapas on the southwest bank of the Usumacinta River, which separates Guatemala and Mexico. The river flows through the Usumacinta Valley, creating shallow benches of flat land suitable for agriculture on either side. Steep embankments with deep ravines lead away from the river basin. This tropical forest has one of the heaviest rainfalls in all of Mexico.

The name Yaxchilán is the Maya word for "green stones"—the color caused by algae in an adjoining river, the Arroyo Yaxchilán. A number of important scholars visited the ruins at the end of the nineteenth century, including Teobert Maler, A. P. Maudslay, Désiré Charnay, and in the beginning of the twentieth century A. M. Tozzer, Sylvanus G. Morley, and Herbert Spinden. One of the most valuable accounts of Yaxchilán is given in Morley's *The Inscriptions of Petén*.

The ceremonial center of Yaxchilán consists of a number of groupings of buildings, courtyards, and plazas studded with stelae and altars. The major groupings are along the bench of the river basin covering a distance of one thousand yards. The extremely steep hills and deep ravines farther back from the river separate other groupings. On the very tops of these hills, some as high as 300 to 360 feet, are lo-

Yaxchilán and Piedras Negras were two major Maya cities along the Usumacinta River. It was extremely important to the Mayas, as it made it possible for trade goods to move from the Gulf of Mexico up to the Petén and Guatemala highlands.

cated many other structures. These hillsides have been terraced with cut stone, now buried under the forest floor. Buildings located on these artificial plateaus are not oriented to the cardinal points, but instead follow the contours of the ravines. The façades of most of these structures face toward the Main Plaza along the river basin.

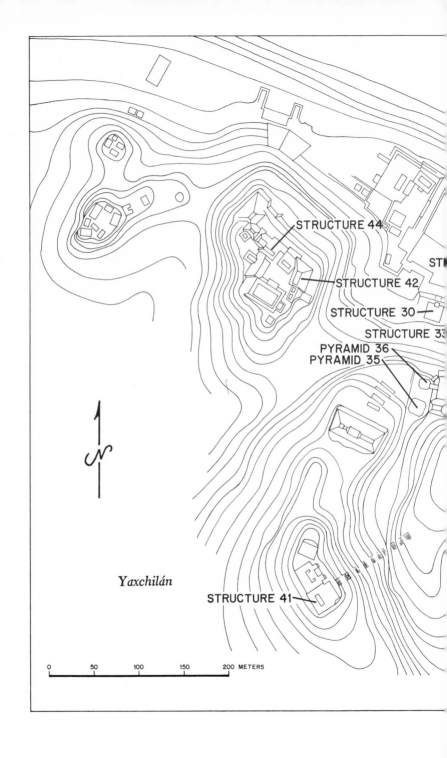

STRUCTURE 44

STRUCTURE 42

STRUCTURE 30

STRUCTURE 33

PYRAMID 36
PYRAMID 35

Yaxchilán

STRUCTURE 41

0   50   100   150   200 METERS

The intensity of the heat and humidity along the Usumacinta River was a factor in the placement and design of many of the buildings. The structures high on the hilltops were designed as temples and residences for the rulers and religious leaders of the city-state. Here there was a cooler and more frequent breeze, sunlight would more quickly dry the plazas and courtyards from the frequent rains, and the elite could escape the humidity created by the river. That part of the city along the benches of the river was accessible to the laboring class of people, craftsmen, and merchants. Canoes and other boats and rafts along the river brought in the produce for the capital city and transported people from other territories who had business at the ceremonial center.

Buildings were of cut limestone, built with high, narrow, vaulted chambers, and many had porticoes. These factors were all important considerations to Yaxchilán architects in planning for rooms to be cool and dry. A similar architectural style is noted at Palenque and Piedras Negras. Constant plastering kept moisture from seeping into the limestone and protected it from plant growth. Painting the buildings and plazas softened the light and enhanced the beauty of the structures for all to enjoy, to admire, and to praise. The high roof combs, porticoes, and other exterior architectural elements were areas where sculptors created imagery in stucco and stone. Inscriptions were located on stelae, altars, lintels, and stairways.

Much of the subject matter for relief carving at Yaxchilán is concerned with warfare, prisoners and their host, ceremonial life, penitential scenes of bloodletting, and visionary scenes. The concern with warfare, a dominant theme in stone reliefs, would indicate problems of political unrest in this extreme westerly sector of the Maya territory. An unusually long quilted bib attached around a person's neck

Among the many fragments of stone sculpture at Yaxchilán, this one depicts a person either giving or receiving a string of beads to or from the dignitary standing above. This monument may have been part of a stela or a panel in one of the walls of a residence.

suggests a type of armor used for combat and is unique to this western area. In a stone relief, Lintel 26 shows this particular item of dress being worn by a dignitary. A similar bib is noted in Jaina figurines, but to date they have not been found in other areas occupied by the Mayas.

The Yaxchilán sculptors enjoyed depicting group scenes on their monuments, which was also popular at Piedras Negras. Yaxchilán had the advantages of contact with the great cities of Palenque and Piedras Negras in the immediate area. However, the style of some monuments and the use of certain glyphs reflected the influence of such distant Mayan centers as those in the Puuc Hills of Yucatán. Yaxchilán composition and carving lacked the grace, rhythm, and proportion of the sculptures at Piedras Negras. However, at the height of Yaxchilán's development, there is a vigor of design and a refinement of stone-carving technique. Craftsmanship in stone carving at Yaxchilán was maintained at a high level until the mid-eighth century, and then there was a decline in technique.

The Main Plaza at Yaxchilán extends along the Usumacinta River approximately three hundred yards. Around this plaza are a great number of structures that may have served as residences, storage areas for ceremonial equipment, and religious buildings. Platforms surrounding the plaza could serve as market areas and places for special ceremonies. Two ball courts are located in the area of the Main Plaza. The one on the west side of the plaza contains circular playing markers, three located in the alley of the court and two located on the benches of the court. The main plaza of most ceremonial centers had ball courts.

On a steep hilltop approximately two hundred feet above the Main Plaza is one of the most important buildings at Yaxchilán, Structure 33. Terraces extend from the

Structure 33 is one of the major temple buildings at Yaxchilán. Above the doorways of this building are niches for sculpture. At one time the temple was given additional height by a high roof comb. Much of this has been destroyed by the encroaching roots of trees. The area has had no major excavation or reconstruction.

Main Plaza to this temple or palace structure, creating an impressive cascade of platforms. When one looks upwards, this building assumes a monumental quality and acts as a focal point for the ceremonial center. The great Mayan lords and their entourage, as they descended these stairs, must have created a dramatic spectacle for the populace who watched from the plaza below.

Structure 33 has three doorways that lead into a long single chamber. This type of room is quite usual for temple buildings. The structure has an extremely beautiful roof comb that runs the whole length of the building. The roof comb is perforated in an open geometric design, and in its center there is a large seated deity. The mansardlike roof was also covered with stucco figures, little of which remains today.

Continuing up the steep hillside from Structure 33 are platforms, terraces, and stairways that lead to a group of three buildings located at the city's highest point, the South Acropolis, 360 feet above the Usumacinta River. On this pinnacle, Structure 41 dominates the hilltop. Here, there are also two additional buildings approximately the same size and having a similar floor plan as Structure 41. On Structure 41 there is some indication that a frieze composed of plaster hieroglyphs was once located just below the cornice. A great stairway descends from the façade of this building to a platform 300 feet below the South Acropolis. The stairway is broken by ten sections in which pylons are incorporated into the architectural design. This esplanade of stairs, platforms, and terracing, decorated with stelae, altars, and other sculptures, must have been an extremely impressive sight.

Directly northwest of the South Acropolis is the West Acropolis, located on a hilltop that rises 230 feet above the Usumacinta River. This acropolis consists of a number of mounds and several large structures which are still hidden in the tropical forest. The best-preserved of these is Structure 44. On this building can be seen beautifully carved lintels to

Hieroglyphs sculptured in low relief can be seen in many areas of Yaxchilán. This panel of glyphs is on one of the steps at the entrance to Structure 44.

167

the three doorways. Also, the doorsteps are carved in finely executed hieroglyphs. In front of Structure 44 were five stelae. The whole platform was terraced to the river basin below. Stairways were flanked by pylons, as were the great stairways to Structures 33 and 41. Yaxchilán had many dedicatory stelae and altars. There were forty-four carved monuments of this type and many uncarved as well. Of the many buildings located here, seventeen of them have a total of fifty-three beautifully carved lintels.

This ceremonial center was one of the major cities of the Mayas along the Usumacinta River. The extent of its territory is unknown, but the strong influence of Yaxchilán on Bonampak sculpture suggests that Yaxchilán may also have controlled this and adjacent ceremonial centers. Today the ruins lie in a blanket of moss and lichens, and most of the city is buried far below the surface of the forest floor. Over the years great numbers of sculptures have been removed from Yachilán by museums and collectors. Recently, there has been much damage done in this and many other areas by vandalism and looting. It can only be hoped that Mexico will someday uncover part of this ceremonial center and provide the necessary caretakers so that more of the world can see another of the spectacular cities of the Mayas.

Bonampak

It seems an irony that the most precious of all pre-Columbian paintings in Mesoamerica are deep in a tropical rain forest in a remote area of Chiapas and are rarely seen by man. The jungle here is covered by a canopy of branches of such trees as chicle and mahogany. This verdant blanket is broken

The plaza area at Bonampak looking toward the grand staircase. The ruins have been only partially excavated, with many mounds untouched in the forest. The distant hill is part of the elaborate platforms that are now covered with soil and vegetation. Structures 1 and 2 are in the right and left foreground.

by the palo blanco tree, which in the springtime forms an umbrella of yellow flowers that shower the jungle trails. This wilderness area is little known and is sparsely settled by a few Lacondón Indians. There are groups of archaeological

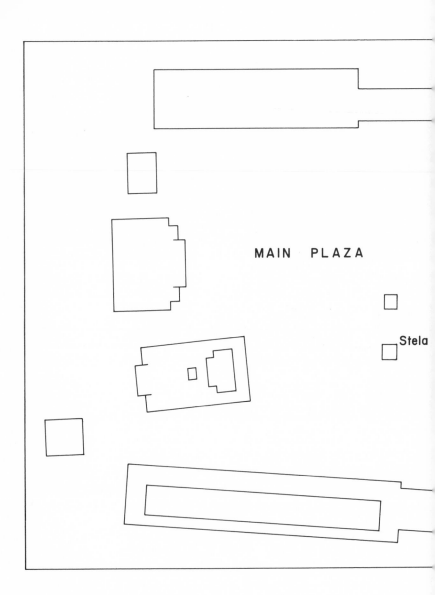

MAIN PLAZA

Stela

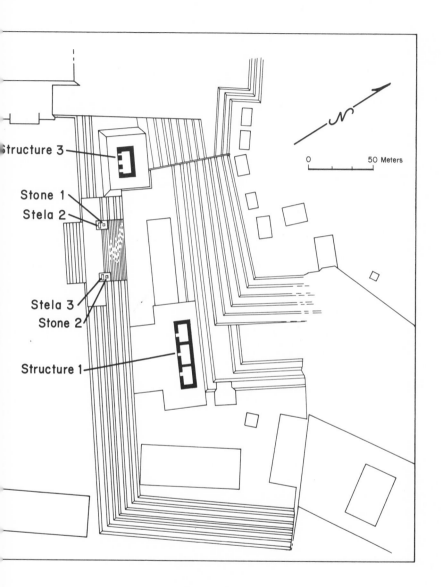

Bonampak
(after Ruppert and Stromsvik)

sites, such as Ojos de Agua, Lacanhá, Oxlahuntún, Miguel Angel Fernández, and Tzendales in the surrounding countryside no farther than thirty miles away.

Although the site of Bonampak was explored by John Bourne and H. Carl Fry on their visit there in February of 1946, they did not see the temple known as Structure 1 with its famous murals. It was Giles G. Healey who discovered the temple just four months later, in May of 1946, and informed the outside world of his great discovery.

On approaching the ceremonial center, a small plaza surrounded by low-lying mounds is first encountered. From here, most of the structures at Bonampak can be seen. They are arranged on platforms on a natural hillside that has been terraced with limestone. The buildings at Bonampak are simple in design and except for Structure 1 are single-roomed. There are similarities in the architectural design of the structures, and in the carving of stone lintels, to that of Yaxchilán. Both Morley and Ruppert have compared architectural details at Bonampak to those at Piedras Negras. However, Yaxchilán was by far the stronger influence on Bonampak and may have had political control over this ceremonial center as well as the many other small centers located along tributaries of the Usumacinta River in the surrounding country. Areas farther down the Usumacinta would have come under the control of Piedras Negras.

The largest of the stelae at Bonampak is Stela 1, now broken into several pieces, located in the Main Plaza. The elaborate costumed personage carved on the front of the stela is in the usual ornate style, but on this particular stela there is little regard for any of the ideals of Maya beauty. However, the beautiful detail of the tracery on the mask form on which the Maya is standing is especially fine and can be well appreciated.

Detail of Stela 1 showing how the sculptor has executed a difficult hand gesture. The long, curved nose, flattening of the forehead, receding chin, and down-turned lip line is typical of the
Late Classic style. It is not unusual to find a fish form used for
the ornamentation of the nose or as a part of the headdress, in
which the fish would be nibbling on a lotus.

Stelae 2 and 3 are located on the great stairway adjoining the plaza and are carved in the same style as the lintels in Structure 1. Stela 2 is a particularly fine carving of an important personage attended by two lesser persons, all dressed in the splendid ceremonial costumes befitting a mighty lord and his attendants. The headdress is important, delicate, and beautiful. The recurrent Maya theme of a fish nibbling on a water lily is noted on the front of the headdress of the right attendant.

The great stairway ascends to the first platform, where Structures 1 and 3 are located. It is important to enter Structure 3, as this building contains quite a large head in stucco that must have been part of the decoration on the façade of some structure at Bonampak. This head lies on the floor of the temple, no doubt placed there so that it would not be damaged further by the elements or by vandalism. Structure 1, as it is seen today, is under a canopy of corrugated metal to protect it from drenching rains. It is in this building that the famed Bonampak murals can be seen. Not far from Bonampak are two additional sites, Maudslay and Bee Ruin, that have been reported to have had murals on their walls. Fortunately, the murals at Bonampak have been partially preserved by a coating of calcium bicarbonate that has been deposited over them by the action of moisture from the limestone. These murals are now over a thousand years old, and the color of the paint in parts of them is as brilliant as though recently painted.

Structure 1 has three doorways, each with carved stone lintels. The subject of the carvings is that of a warrior and his captive. Glyphs are arranged to become an integral part of the lintel design. These lintels are similar to those in Structure 44 at Yaxchilán. Above the doorway is a medial molding running the length of the façade. Over this mold-

Stela 2 at Bonampak portrays a member of the elite in ceremonial clothing. This could be a member of the ruling family of the time. The style of carving shows great refinement and technical skill.

A detail of the head of Stela 2 shows beautifully the style of head-dress worn during Late Classic times. The jade earrings, beads, and mantle are typical ornamentation worn at Maya cities and towns along the Usumacinta River.

Structure 1 is the location of the famed Bonampak murals. The building is covered by a modern superstructure in order to protect it from the tropical rains. Bonampak is a Late Classic site.

ing are three niches that at one time contained seated stucco figures. The upper façade of the building was decorated in a stucco relief, little of which remains today.

Each of the three rooms of Structure 1 are identical in size, and all of them are encircled by a low bench that would be comfortable for seating or convenient for the placement of ceremonial paraphernalia. The walls of all three rooms are completely painted in murals. The composition of the different structural shapes within the room, the masterly drawing of the outline for the figures, and the beautiful rendering of the painting indicate the degree of skill and artistry of which Mayan craftsmen were capable one thousand years ago.

The story of the murals begins in Room 1 with a scene of important personages preparing for a raid on some nearby village. The scene is a realistic one, clearly depicting the action, the manners, the class status, and the dress and ceremonial regalia of the eighth-century Mayas. The lower section of the mural represents musicians and masked participants in a processional. In Room 2 the story of the raid is continued; we see a dramatic scene of the actual raid, with warriors and their enemy engaged in battle. A second scene in the same room could be called the judgment scene, and it is here we see the prisoners being arraigned before the great lords of Bonampak. The mural in Room 3 portrays the sacrifice of one of the prisoners and the pleading of the others for mercy. The accompanying celebration and dance that follow, in which the lords, nobles, and dancers are in their richest of ceremonial garments, dramatically ends the story in the murals.

There are many other scenes depicted in this building. They show activities of the chief, the two women with him, a child, the nobles, attendants, and other persons involved in the raid and ceremony. Each section of the mural is alive with detail. The expressive line used in the rendering of the human figure, the facial features in which great emotion is shown, and the wealth of the ceremonial dress has no equal in any other culture in the Americas. The blue and orange-yellow colors used in Room 1 are brilliant beyond belief. The painting is in true fresco, but there is indication that some color was applied after the plaster was dry. Colors used for the mural have been examined and are found to be mineral colors, except for black.

The Bonampak murals must have been one of hundreds of murals painted by the Mayas. Time and the elements have been the eroding factors which have destroyed most of them. Today these surviving murals remain among the great masterpieces of all time.

VI   Pasión River
Seibal

Guatemala —
Highlands. This wasn't
worth the trip!

The rain forest at Seibal has a lush green canopy that is
sprinkled with orange patches of the beautiful amapola
tree. In full bloom, this tree is like a fire against the blue
tropical sky. The great ceiba trees along the Pasión River
have given Seibal its name—Spanish for "place of the ceiba
tree." Approximately ten miles up the river two palm-
thatched huts indicate the location of the old headquarters
used in 1964 by the archaeologists Gordon R. Willey and A.
Ledyard Smith when they started excavation here. The de-
cision of Harvard University to excavate at Seibal came after
work had been completed at Altar de Sacrificios, which is
seventy-five miles down the Pasión River. Earlier research
at Seibal was carried out by Teobert Maler in 1895 and 1905.
More thorough investigation was undertaken by Sylvanus
G. Morley in 1914.

During Classic times there were many important cities
along the Pasión and Usumacinta rivers. Piedras Negras and
Yaxchilán are two of the larger cities farther down the river.
In the center of each of the cities was the ceremonial area
for religious, social, and political activities. It is this part of
the cities that archaeologists have been interested in investigating. Some of the Maya cities or towns that await further
exploration are Aguateca, Dos Pilas, Tararindito, and El
Caribe. Altar de Sacrificios at the confluence of the Pasión
and Salinas rivers must have been an important center for
trade among the various tribal peoples in the foothills of the
river basin. It is quite possible merchants controlling trade

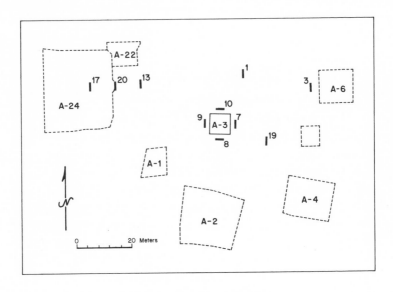

Southern Section of Seibal

on the rivers were members of ruling families from the major ceremonial centers located adjacent to these waterways.

Luxury items from the Guatemala highlands, such as jade, quetzel feathers, and obsidian; salt and precious sea shells from the Pacific slope; and ceramics from such cities as Chamá, Ratinlixul, and Zaculeu would all come by the trade routes over the mountains and into the river systems of the central lowlands. During the terminal phase of the Late Classic Period a ceramic ware called Fine Orange Ware had great distribution from Campeche throughout the lowlands. We can assume the central lowlands had their special craft guilds that created products in demand outside of their own territory. Allspice, cacao, vanilla beans, and other luxury

At Sayaxché this flat-top ferry, manipulated by dugout canoes, takes cars and passengers across the Pasión River. From here Seibal can be reached by dugout canoe or by a vehicle with four-wheel drive if the roads permit passage.

plants must have played an important part in trade. Markets at Seibal and Altar de Sacrificios must have been bustling trade centers.

182   *Structure A-3 is the only structure at Seibal with a corbeled roo*
Originally the plastered building was a dark red. Although t
ruins are very extensive, little of the site has been restored. Seib

as occupied from Preclassic to Late Classic times. However, it
ached a near hiatus during the Early Classic Period.

The density of population was high within the periphery of Seibal, and dwellings with associated small temple structures were found to extend into the countryside as far as two miles. The heavy rainfalls in the Pasión Valley create a constant problem for the caretakers trying to keep the lush tropical forest from encroaching onto the monuments. Stelae are covered with lichens and algae. A brilliant orange alga has been especially persistent in covering the stelae, as noted on Stela 2. Seibal, situated on a low plateau, is typical of a medium-sized ceremonial center. Temples and palace-type buildings are arranged around central courtyards and plazas, but they are not built on the grand scale of those at Tikal or Uaxactún. The plateau is of limestone, which was a readily available material for building. There are indications of two ball courts, one in Group A and the other in Group D. Artificial causeways connect the four major groups at Seibal (Groups A, B, C, and D), all located on natural hilltops. Similar types of causeways are noted at the great ceremonial center at Tikal.

On first approaching the cleared area of the archaeological zone, one is a little overwhelmed at the number of monuments to be seen. At Seibal there has been only partial excavation and reconstruction. The major group here is Group A, dominated by a small temple known as Structure A–3, located in the center of the South Plaza. In Group A there are at least thirty building mounds. Structure A–3 is the most completely restored structure. The temple becomes increasingly important as one observes the four magnificent stelae, one on each side of this temple. Dates on the stelae are all of the mid-ninth century and would indicate that the temple is of the same period. Stela 9, on the west side of Structure A–3, is beautifully carved on the front with a human figure and glyphs, while the sides and back are left plain. The flamboyant headdress with quetzel feathers stylistically places Stela 9 late in the Classic Period. The glyphs have the date A.D. 849. The important person on the monument holds a double-headed ceremonial bar that is decorated with constellation bands and that is held diagonally across the chest.

At the base of this temple building many pieces of stucco and plaster were found, indicating a rather extensive and rich decoration that must have been part of the cornice of the building. An analysis of the total amount of stucco pieces found would indicate that an elaborate frieze, with mythological figures, deities, animals, and human figures, occupied the whole cornice. It is quite possible that other buildings which have not been excavated may also contain handsome friezes. Some of the sculpture on this building was in low relief, while some was in high relief. Life-sized human figures, evidently placed in the center of the cornice on each side of the building, were stuccoed over stone armatures. This type of modeling is not unlike other Maya areas in which large figures were carved in stucco. Structure A-3 has a corbeled roof, the only one found to date at Seibal.

A hieroglyphic stairway is located at the base of Structure 14 in Group A. Hieroglyphic stairways have also been found at other sites, such as Quiriguá, Copán, Yaxchilán, and Palenque. This building may have been a dwelling house for one of the important families.

Stela 13, located a short distance from Structure A-3, is one of the most interesting of the stelae at Seibal. The six serpents projecting from the skirt of the personage depicted on the stela are similar in design to the reliefs on the Tzompantli at Chichén Itzá, carved possibly three hundred years later. Speech scrolls, serpent forms, and costume detail would

At the base of the stairway to Structure A-3 at Seibal is Stela 9. This Late Classic stela, as well as three others on each side of the building, has a date of A.D. 849. Stela 9 shows a very definite foreign influence that was probably from the Mexican highlands. The face is non-Maya. During Late Classic times the Pasión River was already coming under the influence and control of intrusive groups who had moved into the Maya area from the north.

In the village of Sayaxché, en route to Seibal, is a handsome stela depicting a mighty ruler of Late Classic times. His unusual head-dress, ear pendant, necklace, and leg bands are all interesting adornments. A jaguar pedestal serves as the base.

indicate that this stela was non-Mayan in theme, but could well have been carved by Maya craftsmen.

The only monument at Seibal with a standing figure facing forward, and who also has his face forward rather than in profile, is Stela 2. Full-faced stela figures are more commonly found at Piedras Negras, Copán, and Quiriguá. Stela 2 has no carved glyphs, which is most unusual. The person depicted on the monument may be a deity or a priest representing a deity, as he wears a mask on his face; and the headdress is that of a large death's head. The grinning mouth and stiffness of the posture are slightly ludicrous. The style of this monument is unlike any other at Seibal. There is no particular refinement in the stone carving. As one observes the monument today, he sees it covered in a heavy mantle of brilliant orange alga. On stylistic grounds, Morley assigned a date of A.D. 830 to Stela 2.

Group D is the largest of the four sections at Seibal; it has over fifty building mounds. However, few of the carved monuments are found here; most are located in the area of Group A. A visitor can take long walks on footpaths at Seibal, going from one group to the other, and see many stelae and mounds of unexcavated buildings. A good hike along one of the trails will bring you to a circular platform and near it an unusual round altar decorated with jaguar heads on the side rim. This large monolithic stone is supported by a pedestal consisting of three stone monkeys.

Seibal, like Altar de Sacrificios, had a very long history. There is evidence of occupation from the Middle Preclassic Period continuing at both sites until Late Classic times. By the end of Late Preclassic times Seibal was an extensive ceremonial center. It reached a hiatus during the Early Classic Period and may have been abandoned for a time. Between A.D. 500 and 690 there is no indication of occupation. Again,

Stela 2 at Seibal is non-Maya in style. There is some similarity between this stela and those found recently at Xochicalco in the Mexican highlands. In the wet, tropical jungles of the Petén it is not unusual to see these stelae covered with a bright orange alga.

during the Late Classic Period there was a burst of creative activity in construction of buildings and monuments. These are the structures we see today. Dated monuments at Seibal indicate construction continued a little over one hundred years beyond that at Altar de Sacrificios. Both ceremonial centers were highly influenced by Mexican ideas during these latter years of activity, and this is reflected in their art. We see the use of speech scrolls, serpent motifs, and other non-Mayan symbols. Even the facial features on the stelae are those of foreign-looking men. Fine Orange pottery, found at both Seibal and Altar de Sacrificios, indicates trade or occupation in this area by non-Mayan people. Seibal was at its peak between A.D. 830 and 890, and by A.D. 930 the site was abandoned.

The next two centuries witnessed one Mayan area after another, from the Pacific slope into the Guatemala highlands, the periphery of the southern lowlands, and finally the northern Maya area of Yucatán, falling to invading groups from Mexico.

VII Guatemala Highlands
Kaminaljuyú–Zaculeu–Nebaj

The Guatemala highlands, composed of a rugged mountain range that stretches from the Mexican border to El Salvador, encompasses some of the most beautiful scenic territory in all of Central America. Volcanic peaks, some active, are reflected in the many lakes along the range. Present-day Indian villages have maintained an economy, an architecture, and a way of life little changed since the Spanish Conquest. The regional dress of the Indians is by far the most colorful in all the Americas. Clothing has to be warm, especially during the chilly winter nights when frost can occasionally be seen in the villages high in the mountains. The altitude for most of the villages is between forty-five hundred and sixty-five hundred feet.

Even though burros are now sometimes used as beasts of burden, one is more apt to see heavy loads tied by tump-lines on the backs of Indians walking up and down mountain trails or roadways. The Indians are a stocky, sturdy people, proud of their family, their village, and their heritage.

The Guatemala highlands have been the home of these Maya Indians since Preclassic times. There are many ceremonial centers here, some of which reached an apogee early in Maya civilization while others are of a very late Postclassic date. In the highlands there are over one hundred archaeological sites, of which only a few have been uncovered. Kaminaljuyú, on the outskirts of Guatemala City, was one of the largest urban centers during the Early Classic Period, and it may have had a population as large as fifty thousand

191

Kaminaljuyú was an extremely important commercial center during the Late Preclassic and Early Classic period. Since most of the center was constructed of adobe and pumice, little remains of Kaminaljuyú to see today. Most of the excavations are under

he ground in tunnels. The mounds visible in the foreground are till unexcavated. Footpaths lead to various sections where ex-avation has been in progress. In the distance is Guatemala City, vhich has been built over a large part of Kaminaljuyú.

people. However, construction at Kaminaljuyú had started in Preclassic times and by the end of that era a large city had been established. Over two hundred mounds and thirteen ball courts, all of which had been built of adobe, date from this period. Sculpture and pottery reached a level of development not equaled at other areas of the highlands during the Late Preclassic Period. Large stone carvings found here are reminiscent of Izapa-style sculptures, well known along the Pacific slope and in southern Mexico. Sculptured boulders similar to some found at Monte Alto suggest the existence of an even earlier active ceremonial center at Kaminaljuyú, possibly as early as the Middle Preclassic Period (800–300 B.C.).

During the Early Classic Period (A.D. 300–600) Kaminaljuyú came under the influence of, and may have been conquered by, the Teotihuacán people from the Mexican highlands. Their influence is especially noted in architecture and pottery. Building stones were made of carefully cut pumice, set in an adobe mortar, and the surface was then plastered and painted. Because of the use of perishable materials, especially adobe, little remains to be seen at Kaminaljuyú today except dirt mounds and underground tunnels containing the strata tests and excavations of the archaeologists. Spreading Guatemala City now encompasses most of the existing mounds. Since Kaminaljuyú was the largest of the Mayan sites in the highlands, a tremendous number of artifacts—especially pottery, jade, pyrite plaques, and many other objects placed in caches—have been recovered. Some of these objects have stylistic similarities to the Classic Veracruz culture, especially the pyrite-encrusted plaques.

Kaminaljuyú had its great florescence in the Late Preclassic Period. During Classic times no important ceremonial centers were built in the Guatemala highlands. The flowering of the Maya culture had passed by that time to the lowlands at such sites as Tikal, Piedras Negras, Yax-chilán, and Palenque. Copán and Quiriguá retained their power in the southern extremities of the lowlands during Late Classic times, while Uxmal, Sayil, Labná, and Kabah reached an apogee in the Puuc Hills area of Yucatán.

Zaculeu, a compact ceremonial center located approximately two miles from Huehuetenango, was restored in

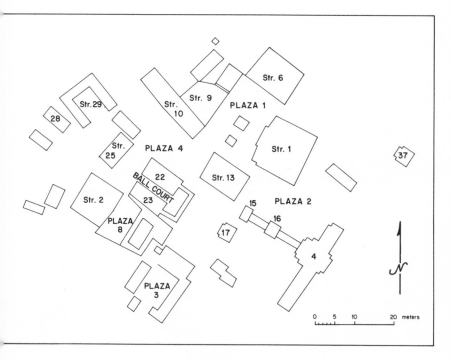

Zaculeu
(after Dimick)

1946–47 under the auspices of the United Fruit Company. Richard B. Woodbury and Aubrey S. Trik, in their notable work, *The Ruins of Zaculeu, Guatemala*, record excavations and reconstructions here. This ceremonial center, like many in the Guatemala highlands, is not outstanding in architecture or monumental sculpture when compared to the lowland Maya cities. In Classic times both Zaculeu and Nebaj were contemporary with Kaminaljuyú and had certain characteristics in common. Their craftsmen executed some of the finest pyrite plaques and jade carvings in the Maya area. Zaculeu and Nebaj continued to be active through the Postclassic Period and up to the Spanish Conquest.

Located in the Huehuetenango Valley, the site of Zaculeu is surrounded by misty mountain ranges creating a soft green veil over the entire countryside. Elevation is sixty-five hundred feet, necessitating warm clothing and well-built houses, for frost is not uncommon. The valley is a fertile one and has enough rainfall to produce two crops of corn a year. Topsoil is dark and loamy and rests on a subsoil of clay, a great asset for adobe construction. At one time this mountainous area was heavily forested, but the forests have been cut back; they are now government-controlled to ensure the provision of sufficient wood for the Indians to build their houses and for their fuel needs. Just to the west of the ceremonial center is a small stream, the Río Selegua, which provides the water required by the local farmers. Unfortunately, no study has been made of the house mounds of pre-Conquest times, which would enable archaeologists to determine the population pattern and its density. Valleys and sloping hills were most likely used for village compounds, much as they are today.

During Captain Pedro de Alvarado's conquest of Guatemala, Zaculeu was one of many small centers that came un-

Structure 1 dominated the Main Plaza at Zaculeu. This temple structure is the highest one here. In the foreground are two small platforms that may have been used for dance, oratory, or music. These types of structures were used during Postclassic times.

der his ruthless attack. He was merciless in his attempts to take the town. Indians on foot with bows and arrows were no match for the Spaniards on their horses and armed with guns. The Indians, under chief Caibil Balam, finally had to surrender in 1525. However, they showed great fortitude in holding off the Spaniards for several months before they were forced to surrender.

The restored portion of the Zaculeu ceremonial center is not very large. Architecture is extremely plain. There is, however, a pleasing variation in the shapes of buildings, the platforms used for superstructures, and the placement of buildings. Seemingly, little alignment to the cardinal points, as noted in most Classic sites, is evident here. There is no indication of roof combs, moldings, bas-reliefs, stucco-decorated piers, or the use of corbeled arches common at other Mayan cities. Of the many buildings excavated, only Structure 13 has any indication of painted plaster. As many as twelve superimpositions have been discovered at Zaculeu, indicating construction from the end of Early Classic times until the Conquest. In all, there are forty-three structures at Zaculeu arranged around plazas and courtyards.

Structure 1 is an impressive temple and is the largest building here, having seven superimpositions and a height of just over thirty-nine feet. Since the reconstruction of Zaculeu was completed in a time span that was relatively short for such an undertaking, little excavation could be done. However, trenches dug by archaeologists into the interior of the structure indicate the number of superimpositions. The façade of the last superimposition for Structure 1 has eight terraces and is broken by a double stairway with a medial ramp on the five lower terraces. The temple has three doorways supported by two square columns. Both round and square columns were used on façades of structures at Zaculeu.

The best-preserved building at Zaculeu is Structure 4, an unusually long building having north and south wings. A pillared portico the length of the structure, with benches along the wall at the rear, suggest that its function could have been for the review of festivals and ceremonies in the adjoining plaza (Plaza 2). A similar type of porticoed gallery is found in Plaza 4 (Structure 10). This singularly long building could also have been used by the ruling elite to see festivals, dances, musicals, or religious ceremonies.

Structure 13 faces Plaza 1 and may have been a temple

Structure 13 may have been used as a ceremonial chamber or as a residence for the elite of Zaculeu. In the distance can be seen the ball court. After the buildings were restored at Zaculeu, they were painted white. However, the original paint color would have been quite different.

building, since it has only a single room that is hardly suitable for habitation. Five superimpositions are noted under this structure, the last constructed just prior to the Spanish Con-

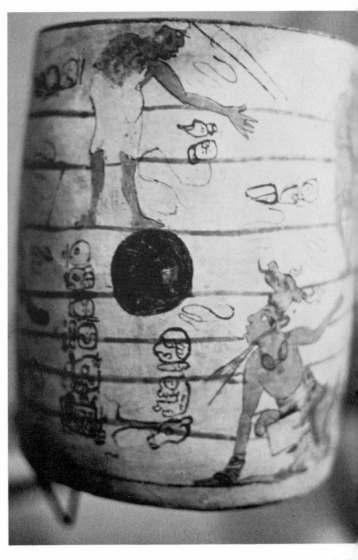

Narrative ceramics depicting ceremonial scenes, deities, and the *elite of Maya society represent a most important phase of ceramic*

re development during Late Classic times. This particular
rrative scene portrays a ball game in action. Courtesy The
nerican Museum of Natural History.

quest. The building is architecturally the most distinctive at the site. Bands of green, red, and blue paint were observed on the piers between the doorways.

The ball court, which has been reconstructed, is a small one with no indication of the rings or markers used for the game. However, these could have been painted directly onto the plaster benches and alley of the court. Superstructures were placed on either side of the court, in a way similar to those at Copán, but only the foundations are here today, giving us little indication of their function or exact dimension. In excavating deeper into the ball court, an earlier, smaller court was discovered under the present one.

With the great number of burials and caches excavated at Zaculeu, much can be learned about burial customs, home industries, trade items, and the chronology of artifacts. Excavations carried out at the sites of Nebaj, Chamá, and Ratinlixul, which lie to the northeast of the Zaculeu mountain range, have also produced a wealth of material that gives us a better insight in regard to the daily life of the times. The superb paintings on the Late Classic pottery at Chamá and Ratinlixul are narrative in form, showing many scenes of the ceremonial life of the people and the nature of their mythical deities. Because of their proximity to the Petén area, they are related stylistically to the Maya lowland pottery rather than to the Guatemala highlands. The brilliant brush strokes used to execute the physical contours of the Maya lords reach a zenith in the Chamá vases, masterpieces of the Maya civilization.

At Zaculeu there was only one really great burial tomb and that was located under Structure 1, the major temple here. Burials at Zaculeu were highly varied. Bodies were interned in vaults, cists, and urns, with cremation common toward the end of the period. There were no particular burial customs related to age or sex, and bodies were placed in both extended and flexed positions. The extended position was used more commonly in the beginning of the Late Classic Period. Urn burials at Zaculeu are noted in Postclassic times only, but so far only six have been found here. The urns were cut at the top so as to place the body in a flexed position and then the urn was tied together. Human sacrifice was practiced; we become aware of this when we see other persons accompanying the dead, especially in the more important burials. Types of burial in Zaculeu can be seen in the little museum adjoining the archaeological zone.

Plaques of pyrite, mounted on slate backs, have been found in great numbers at Zaculeu, Kaminaljuyú, and Nebaj. Thirty-three of these plaques were found in Structure 1 at Zaculeu. Plaques of this type have a wide distribution. It is quite possible the Guatemala highlands was the center of the industry. Craftsmanship involved in making a plaque is technically remarkable. Pyrite is a very hard mineral, as hard as jade. The difficulty in working with pyrite is its lack of cohesion; it has a tendency to crumble. For this reason surfaces are mosaics made of small pieces of pyrite cut and fitted together. On some of these plaques, the mosaic lines are so accurate they are hardly discernible. The pyrite takes on a very high metallic polish that can be quite blinding in the sun. Because of perforations on either side of the plaques, it is believed they were suspended from the neck and worn by chiefs or priests for ceremonial occasions. They may have had magical or religious significance. Because of the uneven surface, it is hardly possible they were used as mirrors. Not too many of these plaques have been found in good condition, as oxidization tends to disintegrate the mineral. However, some of the slate backs on which the pyrite was mounted are carved in beautiful relief designs, many of them in the typical Classic Veracruz style. Many of the ceremonial centers in the Guatemala highlands were influenced first by Teotihuacán in the Early Classic Period, and later by Veracruz, typified by the site of El Tajín, during the Late Classic Period.

Although gold and metal alloys were made into objects of great beauty in South America as early as 500 B.C., metals and the techniques of working with them did not reach Mesoamerica until Postclassic times, fifteen hundred years later. Most of the Mayan area has limestone, and metals are not found in this type of stone. Gold and copper objects found at Zaculeu were probably trade pieces from Panama or Costa Rica. Metal objects as well as Plumbate pottery have been found in burials at this archaeological site. Plumbate pottery, made from a clay that gives a metallic iridescence, was popularly traded during Early Postclassic times, and it becomes an important aid in dating other objects found with it. Some Plumbate pottery has a shiny surface resembling glaze. However, a glaze was never used in Mesoamerica in pre-Spanish times.

Although some jade pieces were found in both caches and burials at Zaculeu, they were not of the quality noted in the great jade centers of Kaminaljuyú or Nebaj. Nebaj is the only Mayan site that has been scientifically excavated to get a chronology of the jade styles. Some of the finest pieces of Mayan jade were carved here and, indeed, it may have been a center for the industry. Sources of jade have been found at Manzanal, and boulders, stones, and pebbles of jade are known to have been recovered from the Motagua River. There probably were other sources in the Guatemala highlands in Classic times, but they were soon depleted and

This seated Maya figure is one of a group of jades found in a single burial at Toniná, Chiapas. The use of the tube drill for the circular lines, the carving of the figure and the background on two planes, and the general characteristics of the facial features would identify this jade as Late Classic. Courtesy The American Museum of Natural History.

have been long forgotten. Beautifully carved jades have also been found at Tikal, Palenque, and Toniná, in Chiapas. A few pieces are carved in narrative relief.

There are stylistic differences in Early and Late Classic jades. In particular, Early Classic jades are designed to retain the shape of the original stone. At that time both the low and high sections of the carving were polished. Facial lines were more symbolic than realistic. During the Late Classic Period carving takes on a very crisp relief, with polishing confined mostly to the upper surface. The body and facial expression is more relaxed and naturalistic. Nebaj jade is distinguished by a mottling of green and light gray. Jade pieces found at Kaminaljuyú and Toniná are more apt to be emerald green or apple green.

There are many similarities between the Zaculeu site and Nebaj, even though they are separated by a mountain range. Their method of burial, their crafts, and their chronology have parallels. It is quite possible that Zaculeu was an important trading center for Indians en route from the tributaries of the Usumacinta River to the Pacific slope. Nebaj was influenced by the art styles along the Usumacinta. Zaculeu in turn came under the influence of Nebaj craftsmen, but retained certain regional traits that were more closely allied to the adjacent Guatemala highland ceremonial centers. Trade routes were important in Mayan history for the exchange of ideas, the diffusion of culture, and the advancement of learning. They ultimately became the routes for advancing Mexican migrations and Spanish conquistadors.

Mixco Viejo

Going north from Guatemala City to Mixco Viejo, one has an opportunity to pass through remote Indian villages and hill towns not on the usual visitor's run. Vegetable and

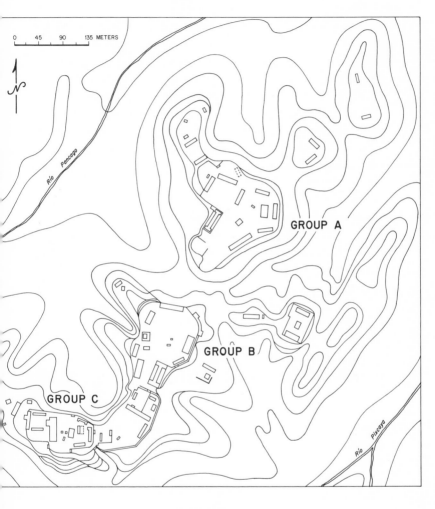

GROUP A

GROUP B

GROUP C

0 45 90 135 METERS

Rio Pancaga

Rio Pixcaya

Mixco Viejo
(after Smith)

flower gardens, terraced on the mountainsides, provide produce for markets in Guatemala City, just an hour or two away. The hazard in trying to reach Mixco Viejo is in crossing a tributary of the Motagua River. Since there is no bridge, a car has to be driven through the river. Should the water be too deep, there is a chance of stalling partway across. Approximately two miles beyond this point, the distant horizon silhouettes the temple platform of Mixco Viejo. During the dry season, golden brown grasses soften the hilltops and cause mauve shadows to darken the rugged ravines. Mixco Viejo is situated on the top of a rugged promontory in the Chimaltenango district of Guatemala and is an ideal location for a fortified city. There are over 120 major structures here, including temple and palace platforms, altars, ball courts, and numerous subsidiary buildings that could have served any number of purposes. At the time of the Spanish Conquest there may have been as many as ten thousand Pocomam Indians living on the surrounding mountainsides. They paid tribute to the Pocomam chiefs. This mountaintop city was one of the extremely important military fortresses, trading centers, and dwelling places for the chiefs, the military, and their families.

Mixco Viejo, like Iximché, is a Late Postclassic site and probably has a history going back no earlier than the thirteenth century. The city was brought to its destruction by Pedro de Alvarado, the Spanish general who burned all the local villages and dispersed the population. The Pokomam Indians were never again to gain power.

On approaching the ruins of Mixco Viejo today, one can appreciate the wisdom of the Mayas in selecting the top of this mountain for their city. A grand vista of the surrounding countryside is possible in all directions. The building program at the site was extensive, and the natural terrain,

Mixco Viejo is located on top of a steep hill in the Guatemala highlands. Only a portion of the city can be seen. The site was an important one in Postclassic times as a fortification for the Pocomam Indians. There are many multichambered structures here, including "palace" structures, twin temples, altar platforms, and ball courts.

with many ravines, was utilized for placement of temples and other structures. The style of architecture has many similarities to that of the Toltecs and Aztecs of Mexico.

Mexican influence in all the fortified cities of the highlands is noticeable. Platforms that served as a base for various types of structures have divided stairways that were separated by medial ramps and flanked by balustrades. As noted in Aztec architecture, the construction of twin temples on a single pyramid was also in vogue at Mixco Viejo. The sunken ball court in Group B, similar to that at Tula, is adjacent to the major plaza and is the best preserved here. Instead of the usual ring used on the side walls of the court, an open-mouthed serpent holding a human head became the marker for the ball game. The only original marker found was removed to the museum in Guatemala City. When the court was reconstructed, cement replicas of the original marker were used.

Another sunken ball court, with the side walls and floor covered with original stucco, is located at Group A near the north end of the ceremonial center. This group of buildings is separated from other sections of the hilltop site by deep ravines. Here, as in all parts of this fortified city, the buildings have no particular orientation, but instead are clustered in groupings according to the terrain of the irregular hilltop. Carefully planned drainage systems for courts and plazas indicate the care taken to ensure suitable areas for military maneuvers and for living quarters. The trend toward secularization in these late ceremonial centers suggest that the platforms in the courts and plazas might have been used for entertainment. They may also have served other functions. It is quite possible that the older use of plazas for religious functions and pilgrimages was displaced in Postclassic times by use as marketplaces. The new ceremonial centers that flourished at this late date may well have been administrative centers and capitals for warring regional groups. Over the years the town of Mixco Viejo grew into a fair-sized city.

The restored sunken ball court at Mixco Viejo is in the shape of a capital I, was stuccoed and painted, and contains replica serpent heads on the walls on either side of the playing alley; the only original marker found is now in the museum in Guatemala City.

Walls were constructed as a protective device, and buildings were enlarged for the increasing population. There are many superimpositions within the buildings at Mixco Viejo today. These may be seen from underground tunnels.

Systematic excavations were carried out at Mixco Viejo between 1954 and 1967 by the Museo d'Homme of Paris under the direction of Henry Lehmann. Excavations revealed quantities of funerary urns, incense burners, and many other types of ceramics. Funerary urns were important, since

Of the many structures (over one hundred) at Mixco Viejo, this building called Pyramid C-1 is one of the few still showing the remains of the original plaster from the fifteenth century. There is no decoration on the buildings except the painted plaster. The style is Postclassic.

cremation was popular here and at many other hilltop sites during Postclassic times.

Buildings were stuccoed and painted, but no reliefs or other decoration is noted here. Group C was probably the most important group on this hilltop, and it can be seen from anywhere in the surrounding valleys. The structures are still covered with a thick coating of white stucco, but fragments indicate they were originally painted. Pyramid C is the most impressive building on this side of the ceremonial center, and it has three superimpositions that can easily be seen by the visitor.

Funerary deposits in Group C included a copper ax and a string of gold bells. Funerary offerings placed in ceramic bowls were present at most burials. It is not unusual to find metal objects at any of the ceremonial centers during Late Postclassic time. One might assume that these objects were imported into the area from Mexico, as this was an important source of metals.

Today Mixco Viejo sleeps quietly in the beautiful country of Chimaltenango. Visitors who make the journey to see the site are impressed by the grand vistas seen from mountaintops of the rugged country, the remoteness of the ruins from the rest of the Maya workaday world, and the traditions of the Mayas that today are still adhered to in the mountain villages.

Iximché

During Postclassic times ceremonial centers such as Iximché, Mixco Viejo, and Zaculeu were in a state of constant change until the Spanish Conquest. This was a period of strife for the Mayas, and a time when regional chiefs were competing

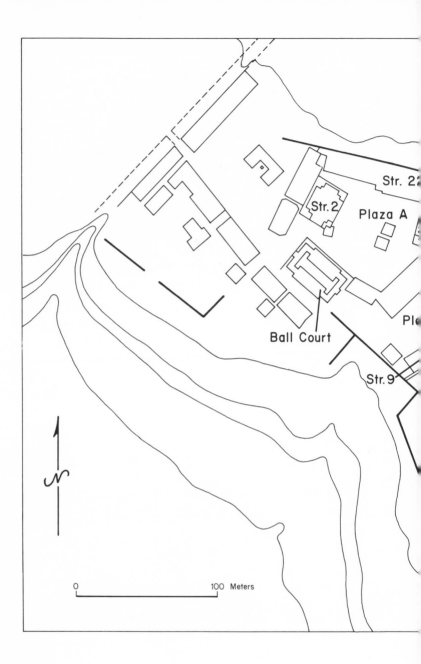

Str. 22

Str. 2

Plaza A

Ball Court

Pl

Str. 9

0   100 Meters

Iximché
(after Guilleman)

for power. Hereditary ruling families were seeking ways to expand their territory and increase their tribute from both the local people and from scattered villages far into the countryside. Progress in this direction would periodically be interrupted by invading migrant groups from the Valley of Mexico or the coastal plain seeking new territory. This *modus operandi* continued over a long period of time. The precedent for this type of expansion existed along the Pacific slope and into the Pasión River district during Classic times. As the Mayan civilization came to an end, migration increased. By Late Postclassic times the Aztecs were conquering all territory surrounding their domain and demanding tribute from areas as far south as Guatemala. Moctezuma had been receiving tribute from Iximché for a number of years and was considering expanding Aztec territory into the Caribbean Islands as well. Introduction of Mexican cultural patterns and ideas into architecture, religion, ceremonies, and warfare was effective to varying degrees.

In the Guatemala highlands, civic centers had to be fortified so that they could be used as places of refuge during wars. New fortified cities were now located on the tops of mountains rather than in the valleys. Because of disruptive Mexican intrusions, development in the arts regressed considerably. Architecture was no longer on the grand scale, sculpture was of little consequence, and pottery was made strictly for utilitarian purposes. Ceremonial centers became more secularized and served different functions, depending on the particular drives of local and regional chiefs. Village life, accordingly, varied considerably from one area to another, reflecting the political unrest, changing religious patterns, and economic uncertainties.

In the highlands small hamlets in the mountainous areas were self-sustaining and had little necessity for contact with larger centers. Farming villages were more common. These were located in the valleys and on the slopes of mountains where ample water supply was available for agriculture and daily household use. Larger towns were more cosmopolitan, and were closely related to the activities of the ceremonial-civic centers of the region. Such towns were bustling with trade and industry. Items from the highlands such as salt, quetzel feathers, jade, cocoa, and cotton were exported. In Postclassic times copper axes and other metal objects, some of gold, were imported from Mexico.

Lineage was exceedingly important in controlling Mayan society. Civic leaders, priests, craftsmen, merchants, and farmers had inherited rights that were passed down from one generation to another. Seemingly there was little opportunity to change social status in Mayan society. Spanish chronicles indicate that this was especially true at the hilltop site of Iximché.

Iximché is located in the central highland mountain and lake district just a short distance from Lake Atitlán. The Indian village nearest to the ruins is Tecpán. Iximché was built as a civic center and a fortress. Most of the buildings were erected around four large courtyards. There are also two smaller courtyards at Iximché that may have been used for religious ceremonies. Terraces were leveled from the natural terrain to accommodate the various platforms for temples and houses. Since the structures had roofs of thatch or of wooden beams and plaster, they have long since perished. Ball courts were common at all civic and religious centers. At Iximché there are two ball courts, one of which has been restored. The sunken court here is of medium size and has vertical playing walls and stairways at either end for use by the players. At Iximché the court alley was slightly slanted for drainage of water. Ditches were then used to

The Postclassic ceremonial center of Iximché is located on a hilltop not far from Tecpán in the Guatemala highlands. Since the buildings were made of perishable materials, only the foundations, platforms, and pyramids remain.

channel the water down into the ravines. Most ball courts were drained in a similar manner throughout Mesoamerica.

Important buildings were constructed of stone and mortar and were then plastered and painted. Superstructures were of perishable materials such as adobe or wood. All plazas and courtyards were plastered and painted, a practice that was renewed at the death of each chief. At that time, tribute

The ball court at Iximché is one of two known at this site. Courts of this period usually have closed ends and vertical sides.

in the form of presents such as ceramics and sculpture and of labor was paid to the family of the dead ruler so that new structures could be built in honor of the new chief. Three superimpositions are noted in Structure 2 to the east of Court A. This building was still in use when the Spaniards conquered the area. Since then some of the buildings have been demolished so that the stones could be used for local construction, as can be seen in the village of Tecpán.

In Structure 2 there are wall murals, now in very poor condition, highly reminiscent of the painting style noted in Mixtec codices. The Mixtecs, located in the Valley of Mexico, were great transporters of their art culture to many ceremonial centers throughout Mesoamerica during Postclassic times. Such sites as Tulúm and Santa Rita Corozal came under their influence. In most structures at Iximché benches are common and served as seats. In Temple II was found a great number of ceramic incense burners typical of those used in the general area of the highlands in Postclassic times. Cinnamon-color cups, known at Zaculeu and Mixco Viejo, were also in use here. Since white-on-red ceramics are also abundant, one can assume that the chronology fits comfortably into the Late Postclassic Period. Although sculpture is rare, two-legged stone *metates* and objects of jade and obsidian have been excavated.

Offerings of decapitated heads and obsidian knives have been found at Iximché, suggesting the importance of human sacrifice at this time. Most persons were buried under buildings with the body placed in a flexed position. In one such burial, an important person was discovered wearing a simple gold crown, beads of gold, and a bracelet of carved bone— not too different in style from those found in the Mixtec Tomb No. 7 at Monte Albán. Although gold has been found in some Postclassic Maya sites as a trade item, it is rare.

Iximché was not an important ceremonial center architecturally, nor did it produce any outstanding works of art. The community and its fortified center were typical of the many hill towns at this time. The structures and platforms at Iximché and Mixco Viejo are quite similar in style, reflecting the strong Mexican influence of the time. Their hasty construction shows little regard for traditional arts and reflects the unsettled status of the political situation prior to the Spanish Conquest.

VIII   The Puuc ɪ.
¯ Uxmal

Uxmal ē Chichen Itza

In its prehistory, Yucatán was submerged beneath the sea. This was true of a large part of Central America and Mexico. Yucatán is a shelf of porous limestone. For this reason there is little chance for lakes or rivers to exist. The only source of water on the northern coast of Yucatán is from subterranean water systems called *cenotes*. The famed Well of Sacrifice at Chichén Itzá is one of these *cenotes*. Rain is rare from the first of the year until late May. In fact, rain is the most wanted occurrence at any time during the year. Population density increases in areas where *cenotes* are present. It is then possible for the Indians to have wells in their compounds.

Farther south in Yucatán, in what is referred to as the Puuc Hills, *cenotes* do not exist. Farmers there rely on cisterns, called *chaltunes*, that collect the rain water. *Chaltunes* are large bottle-shaped cisterns built by the Mayas many hundreds of years ago. They were dug out of the limestone or built into the second story of palace buildings, and hold approximately seventy-five hundred gallons of water. After the cistern was shaped, it was given a very thick coat of plaster, often an inch thick, in order to retain the rain water. Good examples of these two types of cisterns can be seen at ground level behind the palace at Sayil and on the second story of the palace building at Labná. Neither site is far from Uxmal.

The Puuc Hills rise so gradually on the drive from Mérida to Uxmal that there is hardly any awareness of the

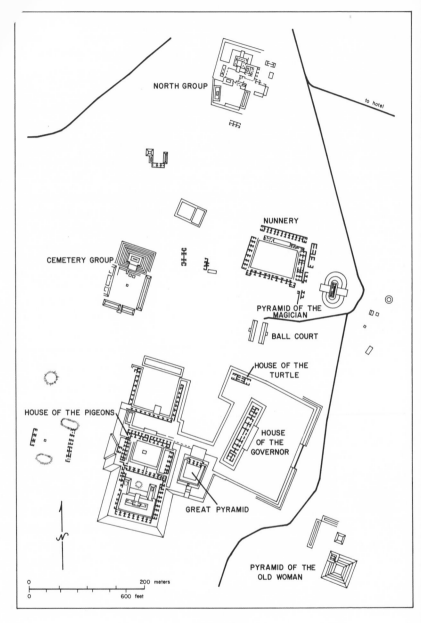

Uxmal
(after Morley and Brainerd)

altitude change from sea level to 350 feet. Nevertheless, there is a slight coolness in the air compared to the heat of Mérida that is much appreciated. The Hacienda Uxmal is one of the most pleasant hotels in which to stay in all Yucatán. From here the archaeological ruins, covering over 250 acres, are just a few hundred yards away.

The master plan for the ceremonial center of Uxmal is in marked contrast to any of the lowland Maya sites in the Petén or along the Usumacinta River. The architects were revolutionary in their design. This spacious, open, flat terrain suggested new possibilities to them. Buildings were constructed on extremely large platforms, well spaced from each other. The plazas covered extensive areas of the ceremonial center. The architectonic relationship between the vertical masses of the pyramids and the horizontal masses of the low-lying palace and nunnery-type structures is one of great harmony with space and with the natural environment. The heavy piers used in the lowlands region were replaced by round and square columns, allowing much more light into rooms. Cut stone decorated with stucco was abandoned for a new method of construction. Instead of solid-core walls, the builders in Yucatán used a rubble core faced with mosaic stone.

Mosaic-stone designs usually are geometric in pattern. However, some naturalistic shapes such as serpents, turtles, masks, and people are incorporated into these geometric patterns. Although the Mayas used mosaic-cut stones in geometric patterns for the façades of buildings in Late Classic times, they were not the only civilization doing so. At El Tajín in Veracruz, buildings are decorated with mosaic-stone patterns. In Postclassic times the Mixtec Indians, who built the palace building at Mitla, used this type of decoration

The great plaza area between the House of the Governor and the Nunnery Quadrangle at Uxmal. Uxmal was built during the Late Classic Period.

quite lavishly. The Mayas at Uxmal developed the style to its greatest perfection.

Mansard roofs, popular in the Usumacinta area, were not used in the Puuc Hills. The Mayas here preferred vertical walls in which the façade above the medial molding was decorated with mosaic patterns while the stone below was left plain. In the development of the cornice, attention is given to a greater variety of forms than at any other Mayan site in Mesoamerica. Some of these dramatic changes in architectural style were also used in the Río Bec, Chenes, Puuc, and Chichén Itzá areas of Yucatán. The culmination of the Puuc style developed from centuries of progressive achievement in the arts.

The use of stelae was also abandoned for the most part, as well as the calendar system using the Long Count, the most accurate Maya system for recording time. Such changes as these would indicate the swing from a traditional, historical-type culture based on complicated religious and mathematical systems to a transitional culture in which many of the old systems were discarded and the mores of society experienced severe changes.

An old Mayan legend tells of a witch who hatched a child from an egg, and this child developed into a dwarf in one year. The dwarf had supernatural powers and was challenged by the Lord of Uxmal to build a temple in one night or face death. He succeeded in this task as well as others, and finally became Lord of Uxmal. For this reason the great Pyramid at Uxmal is called the House of the Magician. It is the tallest pyramid structure here, rising to ninety-three feet. The oldest pyramid, which has not been restored, is the Pyramid of the Old Woman. The design of this pyramid is similar to the one at the site of Edzna, a short distance to the west of Kabah.

East façade of the House of the Magician showing the great stairway to Temple V. This unusual-shaped pyramid-temple complex has five superimpositions. Temple V was the last of these to be constructed. It rests on the top of Temple III. The House of the Magician is ninety-three feet high.

The unique characteristic of the architecture of the House of the Magician is the oval shape of the pyramid from the top platform down to its base. In the afternoon sun the conical shape of this massive pyramid creates some of the most interesting soft shadows to be experienced in observing Mayan architecture. There is an illusion of light and shadow sweeping around the curvilinear surface.

West façade of the House of the Magician. The left corner of the building is Temple I. The façade of Temple IV can be seen at the top of the stairway. Temples II and III are in the interior of the pyramid. This location was caused by later superimpositions.

Uxmal was constructed during the Late Classic Period (A.D. 600–900). The Temple of the Magician has five superimpositions. Here again we are dealing with the Maya practice of constructing one building over another at various intervals of time. The first construction was Temple I, which is now partially visible at the base of the west side of the pyramid. The second superimposition, Temple II, can be reached through a hole dug into the main stairway on the east side of the pyramid. The third and fourth superimpositions have entrances on the top west side of the pyramid. One of these entrances is in Chenes style; that is, the façade is decorated with a large mosaic-stone mask form of the rain god with the doorway serving as the mouth. The Chenes style is noted in some of the earlier buildings of the Late Classic Period at both Uxmal and Chichén Itzá. The style was one that was more popularly used in the region to the south of the Puuc Hills, the largest of the sites there being Hochob.

The last superimposition on the House of the Magician was Temple V, built over the roof comb of Temple III. These additions raised the building to a considerable height. A double stairway was then built around the Chenes façade, Temple IV, in order to reach Temple V. Whether you climb the east or west facing of the House of the Magician, it is one of the steepest climbs among all Mayan ruins. The risers on the steps are especially high. The stairway on the west side of the pyramid has an angle of approximately sixty degrees. A panoramic view from the top platform includes dozens of mounds in the distant landscape yet to be investigated.

Decoration was kept to a minimum on the House of the Magician. The whole structure is unbroken on its facing from the plaza floor to the platform of Temple V except for the stairways and temple projections. On either side of the west stairway a series of large masks of the rain god, Chac, are placed in a stepped position, one behind the other, repeating the diagonal line of the stairway. The use of masks on stairways is noted as early as Preclassic times on the building E–VII–sub at Uaxactún in the Petén, and on Structure K–5 at Piedras Negras from Classic times. A recently ex-

The Nunnery Quadrangle, situated on a high platform, is a
unique type of complex at Uxmal. These buildings may have

been used as residences or as a training school. The quadrangle
would suggest an area for ceremonies.

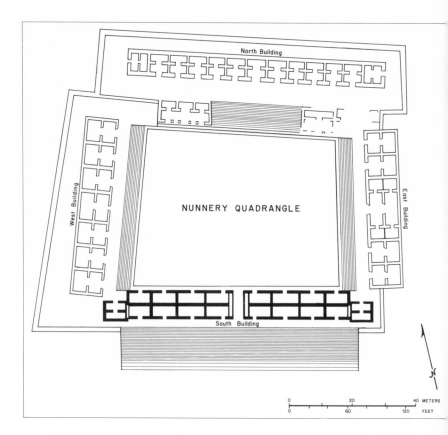

North Building

West Building

NUNNERY QUADRANGLE

East Building

South Building

0   20   40 METERS
0   60   120 FEET

Reconstructed drawing of the Nunnery Quadrangle, Uxmal. (After Marquina)

cavated passage running from north to south under the west stairway of the House of the Magician reveals some of the details of the early mosaic stonework on Temple I. This first building was probably constructed some three hundred years earlier than the last superimposition. One of the moldings for this temple is a series of shaped and fitted stones carved

232

in the shape of the vertebrae of an animal. Below this molding is a row of very short spool-shaped colonettes. Another
molding below this one is carved in low relief with designs of
frets, astronomical symbols, interlacings of vinelike decoration, fish, and human figures. Shaped "toothlike" merlons
hang below this molding in a way similar to the design of a
wall adjoining the Portal Vault at Labná. The most beautiful single sculpture found at Uxmal is a head of a priest or
deity with tattooing on his cheeks, in the jaws of a serpent.
It was discovered below the doorway on the early Temple I
under the main stairway on the west side of the pyramid.
The head has been since removed to the museum in Mexico
City.

From the House of the Magician, the next adjacent
complex of buildings is that of the innovative structure called
the Nunnery. This quadrangle consists of four very long
buildings arranged around a central court. Each building is
separate, thus creating an open space at each corner of the
quadrangle. The decorative style of each building is different,
indicating construction over a period of time. The North
Building of the Nunnery, which may be the oldest, is the
longest, approximately 270 feet. Use of the rain-god masks
in great numbers on the cornice and in panels flanking the
façade of the structure was popular in earlier buildings at
Uxmal. Two other very popular decorative motifs on the
frieze are undulating serpents, conventionalized into geometric patterns, located at intervals along the façade; and
seated persons with bound hands, possibly prisoners, tenoned
into the wall. The north wing of the quadrangle must have
been the most important of the four buildings, since it faced
the entrance to the quadrangle. The eleven double-vaulted
chambers in the North Building, as well as the many rooms
in the other three Nunnery buildings, would suggest that

The North Building of the Nunnery Quadrangle is the longest of the four buildings, and it may well be the oldest.

Detail of the intricate mosaic façade of the North Building of the Nunnery Quadrangle. Mosaic decoration consists of rain-god

*masks, stepped-fret motifs, and serpent forms. In the foreground
is the Temple of Venus with its unusual-shaped columns.*

Rain-god masks, one above the other, become the leitmotiv of the façade of the North Building of the Nunnery at Uxmal.

these structures were used as a large residence. In all, the Nunnery had seventy-four vaulted chambers. These buildings could have housed an institution for the training of priests or the young elite or have been a residence for nobles. The quadrangle courtyard was ideal for ceremonies, as the stairs to the North Building could be used as a reviewing stand.

According to George Kubler, noted authority on the architectural style of the Mayas, the South Building is next oldest here. It is the entrance building to the courtyard and has a plain portal arch. From here can be seen an all-encompassing view of the unrestored ball court and the Palace of the Governor in the distance. Over the eight doors on the inside wall of the South Building are carved native-style huts, each having a rain-god mask over it. These sculptured houses are a regional art form with a great amount of charm. On either side of the Portal Vault at Labná, a site approximately twenty miles away, native huts are also used as a decoration on the stone frieze. For the most part, the mosaic decoration on the façade of the South Building of the Nunnery at Uxmal is a latticework design with little embellishment compared to either the North or the West Building.

The east pavilion of the Nunnery was the next structure to be built; it has more severe decorative lines than any other building here. Not only is the structure shorter than the others, being only 156 feet long, but it has only five doorways, which face on the central court. The restraint of the decorative forms is remarkable.

The fourth, or West, building of the Nunnery was the last to be built, and it shows signs of possible foreign influence in the bold and extravagant use of the serpent and the inclusion of large nude male figures tenoned into the wall of the frieze. Because of the variety of forms used, the West Building probably is the most interesting façade to study. Over the central doorway is a throne with a feathered canopy. The figure on the throne is a symbolic figure with the body of a turtle and the head of an old man. This symbolism no doubt is mythological or religious. As in all the other buildings at the Nunnery, the façade below the architrave is left undecorated.

The East Building of the Nunnery Quadrangle is the smallest of
the structures and the most conservative in style.

The West Building of the Nunnery is the richest in decoration and it may well be the latest of these four structures.

Architects at Uxmal understood the principle of visual correction and gave the vertical walls of the Nunnery a slight negative batter, hardly noticeable to the observer. Such a refinement as this was possible only after generations of progression of style in the Puuc Hills.

Just a short walk to the southwest of the Nunnery is the House of the Doves, so named because of the dovecote

A detail of the mosaic-stone pattern shows the use of convention-alized design forms for the background, with this pattern then overlaid with a bold serpent form. Appearing on this same wall are full figures of warriors and nude figures of men that have been tenoned into the mosaic wall.

decorative device in stone used for the roof comb. This open-work triangular motif is repeated along the total length of the façade. The House of the Doves is an earlier building in style than the Nunnery. Although recent restoration has

The House of the Doves is so named because of the open desig
much like dovecotes that was an integral part of the roof com

f this structure. The front half of the vaulted chambers has com-
letely disappeared.

saved part of the roof comb from collapsing, there is great need for much more restoration here. The north building has double vaulted rooms, not connected, that faced to the north and south courts. Both façades have tumbled down, leaving the roof comb still intact as well as part of the partitions between the vaulted rooms. The portal arch for the building is very similar to that of the Nunnery.

Lintels over the doorways at Uxmal were of wood. When they rotted, the mosaic stones above the doorways collapsed to the ground. Because of large, consistent geometric patterns on the façades of the buildings, it was not too difficult a task for the archaeologist to figure out the original pattern when reconstructing. Since the plant environment in Yucatán is one of shrubs and bushes rather than large jungle trees, there is little damage to the archaeological zones here compared to the rich, tropical area to the south where huge mahogany, ceiba, and chicle trees crushed so many buildings.

South of the House of the Doves is the Grand Pyramid, most recent of the structures to be reconstructed. The pyramid has nine platforms, each having the typical Puuc terminal molding. An extremely wide staircase flanks the north side of the pyramid. The temple at the top has several unique features. Great rain-god masks are used liberally to decorate the structure. These masks have unusual long sculptured projections protruding from between the eye and nose, not noted on other rain-god masks. A depression on the top of the nose, about an inch and a half deep, could have been used for burning incense. The largest of the rain-god masks here is located inside the temple, serving as a doorstep to the rear room. The nose is eighteen inches wide, making a substantial step. On either side of the nose are two depressions for the placement of incense.

246

The corner of the temple on the Grand Pyramid is
decorated with rain-god masks. The tubelike stone
projections between the eye and nose are unusual.

Many scholars consider the House of the Turtles one of the most beautifully designed of the smaller structures in the Puuc Hills.

The exterior walls of the temple have several unique designs, including parrots in low relief, intricately designed molding frames, and other decorative elements. This structure was filled with rubble so that it could act as a base for another superstructure. The building program must have

A detail of the list on the cornice molding where turtles become an interesting decorative motif. House of the Turtles, Uxmal.

been interrupted, as this latter structure was never started.

Just to the north of the House of the Doves is the Cemetery Group. The group is not an important one, but it encircles an intriguing small quadrangle. The small building on the west side of the courtyard has just been restored; it is

The Palace of the Governor is considered one of the most perfect architectural structures in the Puuc Hills. Divided into three

*sections, this great palace is 320 feet long. The cornice is deco-
rated in a mosaic pattern consisting of 20,000 beautifully cut
stones.*

One of two corbeled arches that separate the three sections of the Palace of the Governor. The doorway was closed some time during the latter part of occupation at Uxmal.

A section of the façade of the Palace of the Governor at Uxmal.

raised on a stepped platform. The style would suggest an early date compared to the major buildings at Uxmal. In the courtyard below this structure are four small altars or platforms inscribed with hieroglyphs and symbols that look like crossbones and skulls. Although the "Cemetery" name seems

Detail of the intricate stone mosaic on the cornice of the Palace of the Governor.

appropriate, the area more probably had religious significance and was used for certain rites unique to this particular court.

Located on the northeast corner of the terrace to the Palace of the Governor is a small structure, the House of the Turtles. The building is partially restored. The House of the Turtles takes its place in Mayan architecture as one of the classic gems of the New World, transcending provincial styles. The restraint of the tectonic line, simplicity of the decorative treatment, and unique handling of the cornice list have no counterpart in the Puuc Hills. The list on the cornice of the building is decorated with turtles, with different patterns on their backs.

The Palace of the Governor is considered by most scholars to be the most perfect architectural building created on the grand scale in the Puuc Hills. Situated on an extremely high terrace, the structure faces east, overlooking the great plaza. At Uxmal the progressive refinement of architectural style can be appreciated by looking from the House of the Magician to the Nunnery and finally climaxing with the Palace of the Governor, the last of the extraordinary structures here.

The building is a massive, 320-foot-long structure, broken by two of the highest vaulted arches created by the Mayas for a palace building. These arches are the doorways that at one time separated the three sections of the palace building. At some time in Maya history these doorways were closed by filling them in with cut stone. The frieze above the architrave is composed of twenty thousand beautifully cut and fitted pieces of mosaic stone. These form a design of stepped frets, latticework, rain-god masks, and serpent motifs that move in an unbroken flamboyant rhythm from one end of the palace to the other. The use of a fret pattern is very old, dating back to Preclassic times, when it was used at Monte Albán.

As in other Puuc-style buildings, the Palace of the Governor has no decoration below the medial molding other than on the base molding. Twenty-four rooms with vaulted ceilings suggest that the function of the building was as a palace for the families of the ruling chiefs. At a much later time the Xiu family, of Mexican origin, occupied this building and used it as an administrative center for their conquests during Postclassic times. It was not long after this that the great ceremonial center of Uxmal was abandoned, never to be used by the Mayas again.

255

Kabah–Sayil–Xlapak–Labná

During Late Classic times the Mayas constructed a paved causeway fifteen feet wide from Uxmal to Kabah, a distance of approximately ten miles. Elevated causeways were common at most ceremonial centers. They can be seen at Dzibilchaltún, Chichén Itzá, and Cobá as well as at many other sites. The longest causeway known to date stretches sixty-two miles from the site of Cobá to Yaxuná. Cobá, during Classic times, was the largest of the cities in northeastern Yucatán. The causeway into Kabah is dramatized by the presence of an extremely high, undecorated arch, which has been recently restored. This arch is believed to have been the gateway to the ceremonial center of Kabah.

Kabah, in Yucatán, is the second largest of the Puuc Hill cities. Uxmal is by far larger and more important in size and architectural beauty. Little of the Kabah area has been restored. Pyramids, temple buildings, and palacelike structures dot the landscape for miles, covered with the scrub brush of this harsh, dry environment. Occasionally a deer will be seen in these thickets, still hunted by the Indians for food.

The Palace of the Masks is the most decorated of the visible buildings at Kabah. This palace-type structure has a façade completely covered with 250 rain-god masks, each made up of thirty units of mosaic stone. The building is reminiscent of Chenes-style architecture. The decoration of the façade is monotonous. Carving on the repeated mask forms, all in pieces of mosaic stone, is extremely deep. Shadows cast by the play of sunlight around the mosaic forms soften the harshness of the stone and make this repeated form less monotonous. The decoration extends to cover the façade both above and below the medial molding, and one row of

The Kabah Arch is believed to have been the gateway to the city of Kabah. From here an elevated, paved highway connected Kabah with Uxmal.

the masks extends below the base molding. The nose of the rain god is used as a step to the five doorways—a decided overuse of the mask form. Two cuplike depressions on the masks' noses must have been used for burning incense or

257

The Palace of the Masks is executed in the Chenes style. The
complete facade is covered with rain-god masks that extend from

the terminal molding to the structure's platform. Late Classic.

A detail of the Palace of the Masks at Kabah. The intricate use of fitted mosaic stone creates an unusual play of light in the late afternoon sun.

an oil wick. If so, the gallery of masks must have created quite a dramatic scene when all the burners were smoking. The Palace of the Masks has ten chambers. Each doorway leads into a double-roomed apartment. The building was crowned by an open roof comb, remains of which can be seen today. An evening sunset turns the façade of the Palace of the Masks to burnished gold, an impression long to be remembered.

A footpath to the east of the temple leads to two other major palace-type structures, one called El Palacio and the other Las Columnas. These structures are quite large, but differ from the Palace of the Masks by having rather simplified façades. El Palacio has two stories as well as a high, open roof comb. There are seven doorways in the façade, with two of the wider ones supported in the center by a rounded column that holds the weight of the lintel. Las Columnas, just a little farther on the path behind El Palacio, is in partial ruin. Much of the mosaic stone has fallen to the ground or has been removed for construction, which has gone on ever since the time of the Spanish Conquest. However, enough remains to see the general decoration of the façade. For the most part, banded colonettes and shaped stone spools were used as decoration on both these buildings. On Las Columnas much longer colonettes were also repeated below the medial molding on either side of the doorways. The doors here have a slightly trapizoidal shape, the top being a little narrower.

From Kabah, one of the most difficult, hard-riding, dust-eating jeep trips one can take through any back bush country is that to Sayil, Xlapak, and Labná. Should it be the rainy season, the water holes and flies are beyond belief. However, with competent guides the trip can be made in one day.

The archaeological zone of Sayil is quite extensive, but most of it still lies covered by the dense growth of acacia trees, bushes, and vines that converts this dry limestone country into a jungle. The Palace of Sayil is another of those extraordinary masterpieces of Mayan architecture. Its length

The Palace at Sayil is one of the finest larger structures in the Puuc Hills. The buildings contain over one hundred rooms and rise on three terraced platforms. Late Classic.

is 236 feet, approximately two-thirds the length of the Palace of the Governor at Uxmal. Restoration of various parts of the Palace in recent years has served to establish the true beauty of line, the delicate balance and restraint of

*Second floor of the Palace was designed with porticoed chambers.
The circular columns bulge slightly in the center. Colonettes
play an important part in the design of the façade.*

decoration, and the inventiveness of the architects in handling open galleries, patios, and columned porticoes. The beautiful orange coloring of the limestone façade is no more than a surface stain. Soil that had covered the ruins here for so many centuries contained iron oxide that readily stained the stone.

The Sayil Palace has three recessed stories containing fifty chambers and is approached by a wide stairway that extends from ground level to the third floor. The building is not symmetrical, on close examination, as part of the first floor was built at an earlier date. When the Palace was en-

263

The cornice above the doorway of the second story of the Sayil Palace is decorated with a "diving god" and mythological creatures in carved stone. Buildings in the Puuc Hills are made of limestone.

larged, the old building was incorporated into the total Palace design. Actually, pottery has been found at Sayil dating back to Preclassic times. The façades of the first and third floors are restrained in terms of decoration. The architects were lavish in the plan of the second floor. Here, round columns were used for the porticoes of the eight apartments, opening the rooms on to the deck of the first floor and allowing much more light to penetrate into them. These rounded columns are unusual in that they were carved with a slight bulge. Square capitals hold up the stone lintels of doorways. The walls between the columns consist of a double row of colonettes. Above the medial molding is a frieze of rounded colonettes, a gigantic rain-god mask with exposed teeth over the central façade, and diving gods flanked by short, serpent-fishlike animals. The diving gods were to appear five hundred years later in Mayan history in a degenerate style at a little site overlooking the Caribbean, called Tulúm.

The Palace of Sayil was crowned by an openwork roof comb that was of considerable height. A view of the surrounding country is quite spectacular from the rooftop of this palace. Old Maya buildings can be seen projecting above the dry brush of the countryside. The Puuc Hills form an undulating line on the horizon. Just to the rear of the Palace is a large circular stone catch basin, possibly thirty feet across, for collecting rain water to flow into a cistern.

En route to Labná is the small archaeological zone of Xlapak. For many years it was completely covered by the jungle except for one corner of a small building near the jeep roadway. Recently this one structure has been partially restored and the area around it cleared from the brush. The style of the architecture is quite reserved. In typical Puuc tradition, the lower zone of the façade is left plain. The frieze above the medial molding is composed of a fret pattern and large rain-god masks extending to the corners of the building. On the corners of the structure are engaged columns, unique to the Puuc Hills and surrounding territory. This same type of rounded columns can be seen on the House of the Three Lintels at Old Chichén and on the corner of the Labná Palace. The style of architecture at Old Chichén reveals many influences from the Puuc Hills region. Another com-

265

At Xlapak only one structure has been restored to date. It is
designed in the Puuc style, in which the façade below the medial

*molding is left plain. Rain-god masks and a stepped-fret pattern
are used to decorate the cornice.*

The Palace at Labná is an unusually long structure, built over a
number of centuries, with much of it left unfinished. The cornice

f the Palace and panels on the parament are decorated in mosaic
tone. Late Classic Period.

The Palace has three stories. On the second story a porticoed chamber overlooks the great plaza in front of the Palace. A water cistern, known as a chultun, *has been designed into the second floor. Chultunes of this type hold approximately seventy-five hundred gallons of water.*

parable type of engaged column is used on three of the corners of the Labná Vault.

The Palace at Labná, one of the largest of its type in the Puuc area, is similar in style to the Palace at Sayil. Its construction probably began at an earlier date than that of the

A corner of the cornice of the Palace at Labná has a beautifully executed open-mouthed serpent out of which emerges a human head.

latter, and it went through many structural changes over a long period of years. Parts of the Palace were never finished. Should this Palace ever be reconstructed, some of the grandeur would be apparent. A cistern was built into the second floor to catch rain water. It still holds water today. On the second story of the Palace is an arrangement of apartments. The use of the portico is similar to that of the Sayil Palace, with rounded columns being used in the middle of doorways to support the lintels.

There are many attractive panels and other types of decoration on the Palace at Labná, inspirations of the Mayan craftsmen. One of the finest carved serpent's heads, with jaw fully open and holding a sculptured head of a man, is on the east corner of the façade. Just below this serpent are

Over one of the doors of the Palace is one of the largest rain-god masks ever created by the Mayas.

three engaged, rounded columns. This building is the only one known that has made use of three columns for the corner of the façade. However, others may be excavated at some future time.

A rain-god mask on the adjacent wall of the Palace is in excellent condition; it is one of the largest of its type. Tenoned figures were inserted into the frieze above the archi-

Little of the Castillo has been restored. The base pyramid is still a heap of rubble. A flying façade increases the height of this temple-type structure.

trave on either side of this large mask. The use of naturalistic sculptural forms is not common in the Puuc region. Abstract and geometric motifs were preferred, possibly because it was easier for ordinary workers to carve them. Artisans were reserved for the creative sculptured forms. Where naturalistic forms were used they were confined to tenoned figures placed above the architrave on the frieze or on the roof comb.

273

Adjacent to the Castillo is the famed Labná Arch (vault). On each side of the vault is a small room. On the cornice are two miniature houses executed in mosaic stone. The openwork roof comb is partially intact.

Tenoned figures were a dominant motif on the flying façade of the Castillo, a pyramid-temple structure just to the southwest of the Palace. Although some restoration has been carried out on the temple of the Castillo, the pyramidal base has yet to be reconstructed.

Adjacent to the Castillo is the most noted and finest of all portal arches in the Maya area, the Labná Vault. The vault was conceived as a passageway from one courtyard to another. It would seem the west court must have been the most important, as the arch has been designed with a lavish frieze on this side, whereas the frieze on the east side is designed in a geometric mosaic. The skillfully executed and fitted mosaic-stone pattern on the west side of the arch is a triumph of mosaic design. Two doorways lead into small rooms within the arch. The frieze, on either side of the vault, is decorated with stylized thatched huts, representing a type of house still used in Yucatán today. This important portal vault was topped by an openwork roof comb, a superstructure used on so many buildings in the Puuc Hills. The roof comb here is a stepped openwork triangle. Roof combs in this area never took on the importance they attained in the Petén or Usumacinta regions, where they dominated the temples.

Scarcely populated today, the region of the Puuc Hills maintained a population of some 22,500 persons during Classic times, according to estimates projected by Sylvanus G. Morley. The *chultunes*, artificial wells for the storage of rain water, were controlling factors in population density per square mile. Populations were decimated after the Spaniards arrived by diseases unknown to the Indians. Measles was responsible for the death of over half of the population in Honduras alone. Smallpox, influenza, malaria, and dysentery also took very heavy tolls. In some areas, up to 90 per cent of the Indian population was wiped out. The Indians living in the Puuc Hills today are descendants of the few survivors. Their life pattern has varied little from that of their ancestors during the past thousand years.

IX   Northern Yucatán
Chichén Itzá

The flat, coastal limestone platform that makes up most of the Yucatán Peninsula has been a settlement area for the Indians for over eight thousand years. Indian homes along the road are constructed the same way today that they were in Preclassic times. These oval-shaped houses are built with a framework of slender branches of trees ingeniously lashed together to withstand the hurricanes that blow in from the coast. The sides of the houses are woven with twigs. Red clay mixed with straw or grass is plastered on the side walls until it is quite thick. This clay is then white-washed. A thatch roof of palm fronds finishes the usual provincial house. There is only one door. Because of the height of the open ceiling and the adobe sides, these houses are relatively cool. Hammocks are still used for sleeping. Since the water table is only about twenty-five feet under the surface, most houses have wells. A small shed in the back yard is used for cooking. Although men are more apt to wear typical western dress for work today, women are usually seen wearing the heavily embroidered *huipil*.

For many centuries Yucatán has prospered from its sisal industry. Plants of the agave, used for sisal, can be seen growing for miles along the road. Occasionally large mounds, indicating archaeological ruins, break the horizon. One of the larger pyramids en route to Chichén Itzá is in the little village of Izamal. This site, as well as Acanceh and Dzilbilchaltún, was very active during Preclassic and Early Classic times. Influence of Teotihuacán can be seen in the use of a *talud-*

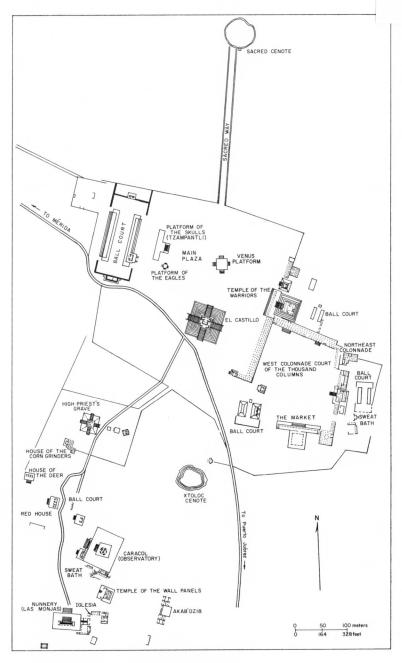

Chichén Itzá
(after Morley and Brainerd)

tablero on the sides of the pyramid. Stucco decoration here is reminiscent of the Preclassic to Early Classic buildings in the North Acropolis at Tikal. Acanceh has a similar stucco decoration. All these sites are only a short drive from Mérida. Yucatán has had a continuous occupation since early in the history of man on the North American continent. Hunting and fishing bands had infiltrated the peninsula by 8000 B.C. With the development of agriculture, and especially the cultivation of corn, settlement patterns were well established during Middle Preclassic times (800–300 B.C.).

During the tenth century a large contingent of the Toltec ruling class and their warriors left their homeland, Tula, in the highlands of Mexico and migrated to Yucatán. They established their capital at Chichén Itzá. For many centuries before this time, Chichén Itzá had been occupied by the Mayas, and many of the large structures seen there today were built by the Mayas during the Late Classic Period (A.D. 600–900). At that time the architectural style was highly influenced by the style in the Puuc Hills to the south.

The Toltecs, on arriving in Yucatán, took advantage of this existing site, Chichén Itzá, and commenced to alter it to be their own ceremonial center. With the extremely capable Mayan craftsmen, the Toltecs were able to fashion a ceremonial center even greater than that at Tula, their former capital. The Tula structures were used as models for some of those at Chichén Itzá. Others were hybrids of Toltec-Maya style, and new architectural forms were also conceived. At this stage of development, Chichén Itzá is classified as Early Postclassic (tenth to thirteenth century). For the most part, the Classic Maya buildings were left without being destroyed, while others were utilized by the Toltecs for their own purposes. Many were altered to suit Toltec

The Castillo, the highest Toltec pyramid-temple-type structure at Chichén Itzá, dominates the main plaza; its stairway faces the path that leads to the Well of Sacrifice. Inside this pyramid is a smaller version of the outer one, which is also attributed to the Toltecs.

needs and tastes. The Toltecs were to rule at Chichén for two centuries before the area was abandoned.

The distance from Mérida to Chichén Itzá is only sev-

Chichén Itzá can boast the largest ball court built in the Ameri-

as. Built by the Toltecs in Postclassic times, it is a splendid
tructure 450 *feet long.*

enty-five miles. Looming on the horizon as one approaches the archaeological zone is the tallest temple here, the Castillo, gleaming in the golden sunlight. On a north-south axis, the pyramid rises in nine platforms, with a central stairway on each of the four sides. Each platform diminishes in size from bottom to top, giving the illusion of a much taller pyramid. The Castillo is seventy-five feet high, approximately one-third the height of Temple IV at Tikal. On the top platform is a temple with a doorway facing each of the stairs, but the main portico faces the north. From here the Toltec priests could view the spacious plaza and watch any processionals to the Sacred Cenote, the Well of Sacrifice, located a short distance to the north.

Only two sides of the Castillo were restored, so that scholars and other visitors to the ruins could see the condition of the pyramid before work began. The Castillo has many characteristics that are typically Toltec, such as merlons on the roof forming a crest similar to those on the serpent wall at Tula, serpent columns, and warriors in relief on the jambs and columns of the portico. Within this pyramid is an earlier pyramid, probably dating from the beginning of Toltec occupancy of the area. The climb up the inner stairway, located beneath the present north stairway, to the temple of this inner building is one of great expectation. It is here that the beautiful red jaguar throne, studded with jade encrustations, can be seen. A fine *chacmool* is also located at the entrance of this temple.

The archaeological zone of Chichén Itzá covers approximately four square miles. At one time it was occupied by the famous Itzá family, who were later to return to Flores at Lake Petén and there hold out against the Spaniards until the seventeenth century.

At the turn of the century Edward Thompson, an American, bought the hacienda at Chichén Itzá and carried out archaeological excavations. His most daring adventure was the dredging of the famed *cenote* in order to reap its treasures. The Carnegie Institution financed extensive excavations and restorations at Chichén Itzá between 1923 and 1943. Only a small proportion of the buildings have been restored. The rest remain, by the hundreds, as great mounds covered by the vegetation of the bush country.

There is no ball court in Mesoamerica that is as impressive for its size or that is as well integrated with the temple and other tectonic forms of the ball court as that at Chichén Itzá. This court is one of the great artistic achievements of Mesoamerica. Not only is it the largest (450 feet long), but it is unusual in having very high vertical sides. At the site of Edzna in western Yucatán, vertical walls were also used for the ball court. Nine ball courts are known at Chichén Itzá, but only this particular one has been restored. The court's vertical walls rise to a splendid height and are interrupted by the large, delicately carved circular rings, placed in the center of each wall, through which the ball had to pass. At either end of the ball court is a small temple. The north temple is decorated with frescoes depicting Toltec life. They can be seen under the open portico of the façade. It is quite possible that the south building may have been used as a reviewing stand by elite members of society rather than as a temple building. The most imposing of the three buildings that face on the ball court is the Temple of the Jaguars. The approach to the second story of this building is by an extremely steep stairway on the east end of the court. The balustrade is carved to represent a plumed serpent. The Temple of the Jaguars is very similar to the main temple at Tula. There are the serpent columns, very beautifully carved, that support the lintels of the very wide doorway. Door jambs are also executed in the usual Mexican warrior themes. The frieze above the medial molding is composed of a jaguar and circular shield motif in a repeated pattern executed in a flat relief very similar to the jaguar frieze on the Tula pyramid. A battered wall is at the base of the temple building, an element typical of Postclassic structures of Toltec and Aztec design.

Within the chamber of the Temple of the Jaguars is one of the few murals extant in the southern area of Mesoamerica. The mural has been badly defaced. However, enough remains to see that the main theme is a battle scene with hundreds of Toltec warriors engaged in the siege of a Maya village.

On the two slanting walls (benches) running the length of either side of the ball court are six reliefs, each forty feet long, placed in panels at three intervals. The subject matter on all panels is very similar. It would seem the Toltecs were lacking inventiveness in not using a different design for each panel. The repeated scene is that of a victorious ball team holding the severed head of a member of the losing team. Blood issuing from the neck is represented by a design of seven snake heads. This bas-relief gives some idea how the game was played, the number of persons on the teams, the clothing worn for the ball game, and the resulting ceremony. The relief carving on the northeast panel of the ball court is considered to be the most skillfully executed.

The first floor of the Temple of the Jaguars faces the Main Plaza and is of an earlier construction than the top temple, possibly contemporary with the inner temple of the Castillo. The structure has an open portico supported by two square columns. The columns and façade below the architrave are decorated in low relief carving.

The Tzompantli is a low-lying platform just east of the

The Tzompantli is adjacent to the ball court and has some fine relief carving on the vertical sides. Known as a "skull-rack" design, the carving shows skulls on poles. The original paint is clearly visible.

ball court. Reliefs carved on the vertical side walls represent a skull rack. Some of the original paint is still preserved. On another panel the Toltecs were preoccupied with a depiction of a sacrificial scene very similar to the one on the benches of the ball court. One section of the Tzompantli wall has a decoration unique for Chichén Itzá. A personage depicted in the wall decoration has a costume that is entwined with

One of the stone panels on the Tzompantli shows a warrior with six serpents wreathing from his sides. Toltec. Postclassic.

snakes wrapped around the waist, with the snake heads projecting from the body. At Seibal, a ceremonial center on the Pasión River in Guatemala, a stela is decorated in a similar manner with six snakes entwined around the waist of a person. A speech scroll coming from the mouth, the dress, and the style of the relief carving would suggest that both these monuments resulted from Mexican influence and may possibly represent the same person. During the latter part of the Classic era, Seibal was highly influenced by migrations of peoples who moved into the area from Mexico. These invasions brought with them political control by Mexican overlords. Although Chichén Itzá came under control of the Mexican Toltecs approximately three hundred years later, the art style is quite similar in this particular relief carving.

Since the bas-reliefs on the Tzompantli at Chichén Itzá were associated with the sacrifice of people, it was expected that excavations here would reveal skeletal remains, but none were found. In areas of intense humidity, and when there is a high level of acidity, skeletal forms will disintegrate. This is not apt to happen in such a dry area as the limestone country of the Yucatán Peninsula.

Ceremonial platforms were popular at Chichén Itzá in Postclassic times as well as at Tula and Tenochtitlán in Mexico. There are two platforms at Chichén Itzá nearly alike, both having stairs on all four sides of the structures, balustrades of feathered serpents, and reliefs on the friezes in panels. On the Platform of the Jaguar and Eagles, the frieze is of these creatures eating human hearts. Both creatures represent Toltec military orders. Platforms like these may have functioned as a reviewing stand for the military, as a platform for dancers or musicians, or as a place to announce the proclamations of the chiefs or ruler. On a cornice molding above the frieze on the Venus Platform is a delicate

The two platforms known as the Platform of the Jaguars and Eagles and the Platform of Venus are in the Main Plaza. They may have been used for dances, oratory, or music. Decoration on the façade is that of an eagle eating a human heart, a popular Toltec theme.

low relief in which a fish is seen swimming in a water-wave motif. The major frieze on this platform, however, is concerned with very large plaques depicting an open-jawed serpent from whose mouth a human head projects—supposedly one of the Venus symbols. There are also other symbols here that have been suggested as being related to the planet Venus.

At a very early hour of the morning when the air is cool, a short walk in a northerly direction from the Main Plaza leads one to the legendary *cenote*, the Well of Sacrifice. The *cenote* is quite large, covering a surface area of nearly an acre. Evidently the well had been used exclusively for ritual purposes over a long period of time, possibly as long as five hundred years. At the edge of the *cenote* are the remains of a small stone structure. It may have been used for ritual purposes during ceremonies connected with the sacrifices here.

Edward Thompson dredged the well at the beginning of the century and recovered many of the artifacts of gold, copper, jade, shell, and pottery. Some of the pieces recovered were heirlooms of previous centuries. Before being thrown in the *cenote*, gold circular disks were purposely crumbled if plain, and if decorated were ceremonially torn in pieces. Embossed and engraved designs on the gold plaques are especially fine in execution. They can be appreciated today only by seeing an artist's rendering of what they must have looked like before their destruction. The subject usually is one of a Toltec warrior subjecting or in combat with the Mayas. Gold was not introduced into Mesoamerica until Postclassic times (after the tenth century). Gold pieces in the *cenote* were imported items from Panama or Costa Rica. Some of the designs were quite obviously executed by Mayan Toltec craftsmen. Copper objects, especially large quantities of bells, may have been imported from the Oaxaca area or from some other part of Mexico. Because the Yucatán Peninsula is a limestone platform, no minerals of this type would be found there. Lime water was an important factor in preserving the copper objects found in the well. The Peabody Museum has the collection from the *cenote* except for

289

A short distance from the Main Plaza at Chichén Itzá is the Sacred Cenote, often referred to as the Well of Sacrifice. This cenote has proved to be a treasure house of artifacts thrown into the well over several centuries.

The Temple of the Warriors at Chichén Itzá is Toltec in design. A structure similar to this is located at the northern Toltec capital, Tula. However, the latter is poorly executed when compared to the temple at Chichén Itzá. Postclassic.

a few pieces which are at the Museum of Anthropology in Mexico City.

From a narrow path around the edge of the *cenote*, a picturesque view is seen of the well and the pathway leading to the Castillo that rises above the horizon in the distance.

The Temple of the Warriors, adjacent to the Castillo, is an impressive Toltec Building that is similar to the Pyramid of Quetzalcóatl (Building B) at Tula. However, the

Two feathered-serpent columns hold up the porticoed arch to the Temple of the Warriors. The heads are fanciful, but beautifully executed.

Toltecs at Chichén Itzá created much larger, more finely decorated, and technically more beautiful buildings than those at the northern Toltec capital, Tula.

The Temple of the Warriors rises in four platforms and is flanked on the west and south sides by approximately two hundred round and square columns. The square columns are carved in low relief, repeating a much overused Toltec theme, the warrior. In a few instances the original color can be seen painted on the columns.

Detail of the serpent heads at the base of the feathered-serpent columns.

The Temple of the Warriors is approached by a broad stairway with a plain, stepped ramp on either side. These ramps are surmounted with figures of standard-bearers for the purpose of holding flags. As far as we know, sculptured standard-bearers were not used by the Mayas, and at Chichén Itzá they are considered definitely a Toltec trademark. Serpent columns, carved to a monumental scale, are used to hold the lintels above the doorways. The roof of wood and stucco perished centuries ago. The façade of the building is quite plain, broken by an occasional rain-god-mask panel or an open-jawed serpent holding a human head.

Beneath this temple is a much earlier one which may have been built as one of the first constructions of the Toltecs after their arrival. The importance of the inner structure is in the preservation of the original color of the stone columns. The walls were painted with murals and fortunately were sketched and photographed before they started to disintegrate from exposure to air when the temple was first opened.

Several sculptural figures referred to as *chacmools* have been found at Tula and at Chichén Itzá. There is a fine one in the inner temple of the Castillo, and another at the top of the stairway to the Temple of the Warriors. This type of sculpture, a man leaning back in a rather uncomfortable position on his elbows, is not an original idea of the Toltecs. Similar types of altars have been noted as far south as Costa Rica. Nevertheless, the Toltec artists defined a specific style for the *chacmool* and used this sculptural form in many of the buildings here at Chichén Itzá. The monument may have been used as a place to leave offerings to the priests or to the gods. It also could have been used as an oil basin for the purpose of a ceremonial fire.

On the south side of the first platform on the Temple

of the Warriors is an engaging frieze of bears, jaguars, and eagles which breaks the monotony of the horizontal bands of the platforms.

A large altar-type platform supported by nineteen Atlantean figures is located to the rear of the upper Temple of the Warriors. This altar originally was located inside the inner temple beneath the present structure. When the superimposition was built, the altar was removed to this topmost position of the building. Atlantean figures, holding up altars and ceremonial seats, are another type of sculptured figure often used by the Toltecs. These little figures, with upraised arms, are seen in great numbers at Chichén Itzá. The earliest known use of Atlantean figures is on a sculpture excavated at Potrero Nuevo, Veracruz, that is of Late Preclassic date, carved approximately fifteen hundred years before the Toltecs found it a convenient sculptural form. The Toltec carving does not have the creative bloom or the fine execution of this unique Potrero Nuevo treasure. The two largest Atlantean figures at Chichén Itzá can be seen by taking the dirt road to Old Chichén. However, there are no taller Atlantean figures than the ones on top of the Pyramid of Quetzalcóatl at Tula. These high columns were cut in sections and then doweled together. It is quite possible that the large, sculptured water deity now located at the entrance of the Museum of Anthropology in Mexico City was used as an Atlantean figure. This monumental monolithic sculpture was produced by the Teotihuacán civilization during Early Classic times.

Steam baths are common in parts of the Maya world today. The tradition is a long one that possibly extends back in Maya history for some two thousand years. The function of the baths was not only to cleanse the body, but to serve for ritual purposes also, and they had medical significance as well. At Chichén Itzá a steam bath can be seen just a few hundred feet to the southeast of the Temple of the Warriors. Nearby is the so-called "Market Place," which has the tallest columns in this archaeological zone. Another bath is on the south side of the Caracol.

Chichén Itzá is separated into two parts by a commercial highway leading to Puerto Juárez. On the west side of the highway a trail leads to the older section of Chichén Itzá, where most of the buildings were built by the Mayas in Late Classic times, possibly three to six hundred years before the Toltec arrival. The Nunnery, the Iglesia, and the Red House all fall in this category. The Red House is built on an unusually high platform for the small size of the structure. It is the only reconstructed building here that has a flying façade, decorated with rain-god masks, as well as a roof comb of stepped frets. Alongside the platform of the Red House is an unusual tree with brilliant orange blossoms and round leaves, called *ciricole* locally. These leaves feel like sandpaper and have been used by the Mayas over the centuries for polishing and cleansing their pottery and wooden objects.

Names of buildings, such as Castillo, Nunnery, Caracol, and Iglesia, have nothing to do with their original function. The conquistadors "dubbed" them after similar types of buildings in Spain. They had been abandoned several centuries before the arrival of Cortés and his army, and their functions were unknown to the Spaniards.

There has always been some question as to how much of the Astronomical Observatory (Caracol) was built by the Mayas before the Toltec arrival, and the degree to which it was altered or additions were made at a later time. The room at the top of the circular tower is approached by a circular stairway. From here, sight lines are obtained for the equinoxes, the summer solstice, and the cardinal directions. The circular tower and the incensories around the Caracol plat-

The Red House at Chichén Itzá is raised by a very high platform. Both a flying façade and a roof comb give the building additional height. Executed in the Puuc style, this structure and many others at Chichén Itzá are Maya. They are Late Classic.

form suggest that these are Toltec additions. The balustrade on the main stairway is in the form of a serpent, and its execution in quite deep relief is especially realistic.

297

The Observatory, sometimes called the Caracol, has been accred
ited to the Toltecs who dominated Chichén Itzá in Postclassic

times. The structure may have been used for astronomical cal-culations.

This palace-type structure, named the "Nunnery" by the Span-

iards, is the largest at Chichén Itzá, and is Late Classic Maya.

From the Caracol, a sweeping view of the large palace-type structure called the Nunnery, the Iglesia, and the Temple of the Wall Panels can be viewed. The Nunnery has not been completely restored, but it is quite apparent that the structure is Mayan rather than Toltec, as it shows definite Puuc influence. Over a period of time many alterations and additions were made. As the building stands today, it is over two hundred feet long and rises on platforms to three stories above the plaza floor. The round corners of the major platform, that now serves as a base for the second floor, are similar in style to those on the platform for the Red House. A later addition to the east wing of the Nunnery is in the Chenes style—the only structure in this style excavated at Chichén Itzá to date. The style is easily recognized by the use of mosaic-stone decoration both above and below the medial molding in an intricate and rather monotonous pattern of rain-god masks. This pattern is broken by a more interesting panel of a seated deity, framed in a unique circular mosaic frame, above the door. The Iglesia, a separate single-roomed temple adjacent to the Annex, is again in the Puuc style—more commonly used by the Mayas in Yucatán during Late Classic times.

A good hike from the hacienda once owned by Edward Thompson over a dust-covered trail into the bush country leads to Old Chichén. Actually, the Maya structures in this area are of the same period as the Nunnery, the Iglesia, and the Red House. The architecture of the buildings is consistent with the Puuc style, and they fit comfortably within the seventh to tenth century time span.

There are many buildings and sculptures to examine and to investigate on this route through a hilly woodland. An early Maya door lintel carved in stone with a plumed serpent decoration, a house dedicated to the phallus, and a so-

Located adjacent to the Nunnery is the Iglesia, a small structure that may have been some type of temple building. The roof comb is quite high and is decorated with rain-god masks. The Iglesia is Late Classic Maya.

called hermaphroditic structure are all encountered on this trail. But there is only one building of renown in Old Chichén, and that is the House of the Three Lintels. This small structure, possibly a residence for a chief and his family, is a classic structure that has a simplicity equaled only by the House of the Turtles at Uxmal. In typical Puuc style, the building is of plain cut stone below the medial molding. Above is an alternating, rounded colonette and lattice-frieze decoration. At each corner is the rain-god mask. Rounded, engaged columns are placed at corners of the building, cut in an identical way to those on a building at Xlapak and the Portal Vault at Labná. The House of the Three Lintels has a decorated base molding of a lattice, fret, and mask design. Very few base moldings are decorated and it is quite unusual on as small a building as this one. There are few small buildings constructed during Late Classic times in Yucatán with a tectonic grandeur that lifts them above the provincialism often associated with smaller structures.

Old Chichén must have been part of a larger complex that was associated with some of the more important structures adjacent to the Nunnery. The Late Classic architectural style at Chichén Itzá is closely related to other ceremonial centers in the northern lowlands, such as Uxmal, Kabah, Sayil, and Labná. At these centers we have the concerted thinking of the Mayas in regard to city planning and religious practices. However, autonomous city-states in this vast area, ruled by chieftains, perpetuated regional differences in the style of architecture, pottery, painting, and sculpture.

Toltec structures at Chichén Itzá such as the Castillo, the Temple of the Warriors, and the ball court are great achievements in architecture, and they mark this ceremonial center as the most important one in the Maya area during Postclassic times.

X   Quintana Roo
Tulúm

The island of Cozumel was important in precolonial times as a shrine for those Mayans who wished to make offerings to the "Lady of the Rainbow." This important deity, Ixchel, was the wife of the all-embracing Maya god, Itzamná. Ixchel was goddess of medicine. Pilgrims flocked to the shrine from near and far, especially prospective mothers. Priests, hidden behind the shrine, answered petitions to the large pottery figure of the goddess. Most of the Mayan temples were torn down by the Spaniards, who used the stones for their own buildings and for roads. Today there is little indication that Cozumel was once occupied by the Mayas.

Tulúm is opposite Cozumel on the east coast of Yucatán in the province of Quintana Roo. The mainland is dry brush country, sparsely settled, with little communication with the outside world. As one approaches the rugged coast, he can see Tulúm perched high on a cliff, surrounded by a great wall, overlooking the Caribbean. Tulúm has never been given much space in literature because it is not one of the major sites of Yucatán. The fame of both Chichén Itzá and Uxmal has dimmed the luster of this smaller Postclassic ceremonial center.

Tulúm was first seen by Europeans when a Spanish expedition, headed by Juan de Grijalva, sailed along this coast in the sixteenth century. In the reports describing the cities here at the time, one of those mentioned presumably was Tulúm. While the Spaniards exploited, placated, and decimated the population over the next few centuries, Tulúm

Aerial view of Tulúm, a Postclassic Maya city that overlooks the Caribbean Sea. The perimeter of the city is outlined by a high limestone wall. The road in the distance leads to a small landing strip.

became overgrown by the dry, hostile type of vegetation referred to as brush. John L. Stephens and Frederick Catherwood, well known for their expeditions into Central America, came here in 1848, cleared and explored the ruins, and exposed them to world investigation.

There are five entrances to the walled city of Tulúm.

Through these portal arches the ruins of Tulúm, covering some sixteen acres, are spread before the visitor. The first shock comes from the size of the city. The buildings, and especially the doorways, all look as though the ceremonial center was planned and built for a group of miniature people from another planet. The buildings resemble doll houses clustered to form a town. The scale is astonishing after the great towering pyramids and palaces at Uxmal and Chichén Itzá. Nevertheless, there is something intrinsically beautiful in the way the white limestone buildings are dotted within the enclosure of the great wall. Most of the buildings face to the west, allowing the afternoon sun to play on frescoes on the façades of exterior walls. On the very eastern side of Tulúm, the Castillo, highest temple-type building here, acts as a unifying force for the city, much as a church does in any present-day small town in Yucatán.

Many archaeological investigations have been conducted at Tulúm, including those by the Carnegie Institution of Washington and by the National Institute of Anthropology and History of Mexico. Tulúm, as well as the surrounding countryside, was occupied by the Mayas in Preclassic times. The only proof of that occupation, however, is pottery sherds. There is also evidence of occupation during the Classic era. However, the buildings one sees today are all of Postclassic times. This is ascertained not only by the architectural style of the structures but by the murals and by the use of fortified walls. The latter are known to be used only at late Postclassic sites.

The architecture has none of the refinements of the Classic Period. For the most part it is crude in finish and lacks proportions that would give the temple and palace-type buildings distinction. At best, the workmanship is extremely careless.

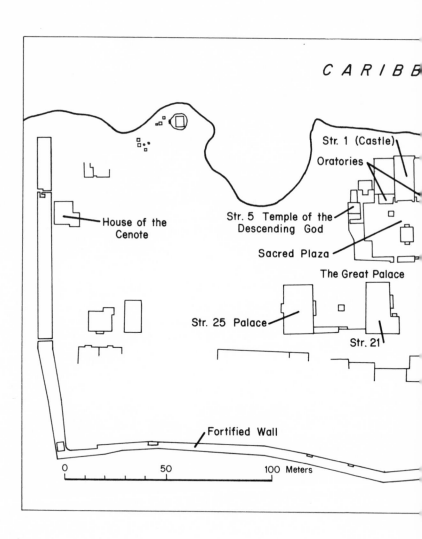

CARIBB

Str. 1 (Castle)

Oratories

Str. 5 Temple of the
Descending God

Sacred Plaza

The Great Palace

Str. 25 Palace

Str. 21

House of the
Cenote

Fortified Wall

0   50   100 Meters

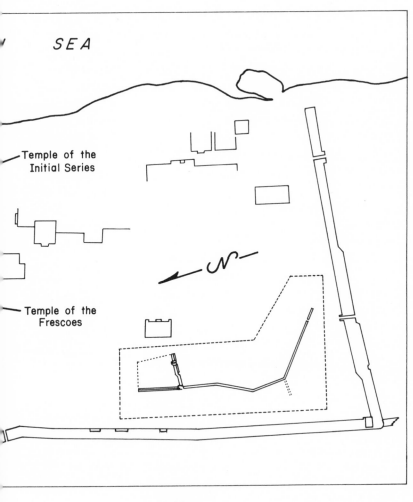

SEA

Temple of the
Initial Series

Temple of the
Frescoes

Tulúm
(after Lothrop)

The ceremonial center, which includes some of the most important buildings at Tulúm, is separated from the rest of the city by an inner courtyard that could have been used for religious pageantry and ceremonial gatherings. In this precinct is the Castillo, Temple of the Descending God, Temple of the Initial Series, and two small oratories. These are some of the major structures at Tulúm. Located on the extreme eastern side of the city, this area is closest to the sea, and the sea acts as a backdrop for the buildings. From the Castillo, the Mayas had a glorious view of the rugged coast below.

A fair-sized population lived in this rather intimately planned urban community, estimated by Michael Coe to have been roughly five hundred to six hundred persons. Like most ceremonial centers, it was oriented to the cardinal points. Throughout Mayan history there is religious and mythological significance to the four directions—north, east, south, and west. Aside from the symbolic meanings, the directions were important factors in Mayan calendrics. The time of the summer and winter solstices and the vernal and autumnal equinoxes determined the work patterns and religious events.

The most important street in the community, which separated the ceremonial center from the palace buildings, formed an axis from north to south. Many of the buildings faced this roadway. Since Tulúm was definitely planned as an urban center, there are parallel streets that separate the various parts of the town. In this respect Tulúm is quite different from any other Mayan site.

The fortified wall surrounding Tulúm on three sides is broken by archways that give access to other communities active during Postclassic times. Watchtowers with a single room are located on each corner of the west wall. Inside the room is an altar. At one time the exterior walls of these towers were painted with murals. Because of the protective cliff and sea, there is no wall on the east side of Tulúm. In great contrast with the Maya Classic Period (A.D. 300–900), the Postclassic Period must have been a time of constant warfare, when ruling chiefs of small states contested for position or territory. Walled towns were evidently necessary, and fortifications of various types were built over a large part of Mesoamerica at that time. In the Maya area fortifications are noted from Mixco Viejo in Guatemala to Mayapán in Yucatán.

According to J. Eric S. Thompson, Tulúm was an important trading center where merchants could route goods from the Caribbean to the Petén and Usumacinta regions of Guatemala and Mexico. The town was also important for intercoastal trade. One branch of the Itzá family, noted for their aggressive conquests in other regions of Yucatán, moved into the Tulúm area from the Petén. They may have been instrumental in setting up these trade routes.

Influence of other cultures in Mesoamerica is deeply imprinted on the architecture, the decorative stucco details, and the wall murals. Toltec influence is evident in the use of plumed-serpent columns on the Castillo. The talus at the foot of some buildings is also an import from the Toltec area. The most important god in the sculpture at Tulúm is the "descending," or "diving," god. Niches over doorways broke the flat walls and offered a place for the sculptured reliefs in stucco. Descending gods have been used consistently since Classic times in both Mexico and Central America. Specific information on their meaning is lacking. However, the Mayan religion encompasses many heavenly deities who watch over and protect the people of this earth. The upside-down position of the deity would suggest that it may be one

311

of these gods. At El Tajín in Veracruz the descending god, in a macabre variation, becomes part of the decoration on the ball court walls. In Yucatán during Late Classic times the descending god is an integral part of the mosaic design on the façade of the Palace at Sayil. And now, three to four hundred years later, the deity becomes important at Tulúm.

Another cultural influence from the north is seen in the style of the frescoes painted on both the interior and exterior walls of the buildings. The best preserved of these are on the Temple of the Frescoes. Resplendent in brilliant murals of this type, the buildings must have been impressive in their time. Against the bleak countryside surrounding the site they would have offered a most agreeable contrast. The style of murals at Tulúm is very similar to the Mixtec codices. Not far down the coast from Tulúm the site of Santa Rita de Corozal also had murals on their buildings showing Mixtec influence. Sylvanus G. Morley, the great Mayan scholar, suggests that a new religion may have been introduced to this coast from Mexico during Late Postclassic times. If this was so, we could assume that some of the Toltec and Aztec gods were assimilated into the pantheon of Mayan deities. On the other hand, the subject matter of the murals seems to be totally Mayan.

On entering the ceremonial center of Tulúm, one of the first important buildings to be seen is the Temple of the Frescoes. This temple has three superimpositions, the last being a second story with a doorway opening on the roof. Over the door is a niche which held a seated figure carved in stucco. Access to the second floor has been destroyed. The façade is distinctive, with four columns supporting a portico —a later addition to enlarge the original building. By the addition of this portico the murals on the exterior walls of the original façade were protected from hurricanes and other

The Temple of the Frescoes is the most important building at Tulúm because of the murals under the portico. Here we see the influence of the Mixtec style. The Mixtecs were influential throughout Mesoamerica in trade, religion, and the arts. Niches over the doorways of this temple contained sculptures of seated deities and a "diving" god.

storms blowing in from the Caribbean. The interior walls are also decorated with murals. Some are quite well preserved. Over the doorway of the temple are three niches in which stucco sculptures, rather crudely executed, were placed. The center one represents the "descending god," and the two end sculptures are of seated figures, possibly of other deities. All

313

Section of the mural in the Temple of the Frescoes. This elaborate mural has been preserved because of the portico that protected the area from the weather. The style of the mural is Mixtec. Late Postclassic.

are in very poor condition. Most of the structures at Tulúm have coarse medial moldings, decorated with stucco and painted. On the Temple of the Frescoes the molding is decorated with rosettes, an often-used motif throughout the Maya area. The façade also has two bas-reliefs, human figures entwined in curvilinear designs, quite well preserved.

314

An unusual architectural decoration on the corners of the Temple of the Frescoes is a stucco sculpture of a face mask that sweeps around the ends of the façade. In style the face is quite similar to a stela at El Tajín, located on the stairs of Structure 5. However, that stela was carved of stone several centuries earlier.

Tulúm was the last Mayan ceremonial center to use stucco as a decorative technique. There can be no comparison of the stuccoes here to the great stucco sculptures executed during the Maya Classic Period. The Temple of the Frescoes, as well as all buildings at Tulúm, was plastered. Plaster hid the crude carving of the building stones and gave a base for the painted murals. Only on the outer plaster do we find mural paintings. This indicates that the painting must have been done just prior to the time of the Conquest.

Most buildings at Tulúm have a very decided outward batter that gives the effect of their being slightly top-heavy. This is especially true in the Temple of the Descending God, located just a little to the north of the Castillo. In contrast to the outward batter of the exterior walls, the doorways have a noticeable inward inclination. Here again, we are reminded of the style of doorways at Kabah and other sites in the Puuc hills during Late Classic times. Tulúm architects were not sensitive to the subtleties or refinements of the great Classic traditions. At Tulúm in particular the walls of the buildings are far from straight. The design of the buildings is clumsy, and the juxtapositions of architectural forms awkward.

The function of buildings at this ceremonial center seems clearer than at other sites. Since the whole town was within a fortified wall, residences for the craftsmen and merchants must have been within the community. It is possible farmers were settled in the surrounding country, but had quick access to the city should there be warfare. Fishermen may have had their own hamlets along the coast. Palace buildings were used as a residence by the important chiefs and their families, priests, and visiting dignitaries.

Within the inner precinct of the ceremonial center, the tallest and most imposing building is the Castillo. There are many superimpositions in this and other buildings at Tulúm, indicating urban growth and development. It seems obvious that the building was used as a temple and not as a "castle" —a word dubbed on it by the conquistadors. There was sufficient room in the structure for a priest's residence, although there is no way of knowing if it served this purpose. A great stairway with ramps leads to the temple, three stories above ground level. A pair of plumed-serpent columns support the lintels for the doorways. As in the Temple of the Frescoes, niches over the doorways contain stucco sculptures, the central one again being the descending god. According to the time and occasion, this descending figure could represent several different deities coming down from heaven. Celestial deities have played an important part in the art of Mesoamerica from the earliest times.

On either side of the Castillo is a very small oratory building that must have been used by the priests for incantations and in making offerings. It is necessary to stoop to enter the little door to this single-chambered structure.

Just to the north of the Castillo is Structure 5, usually called the Temple of the Descending God. The design of this miniature temple follows that of other structures here. The vertical walls are decidedly battered, a cornice encircles the temple top, a descending god is in stucco over the doorway, and the walls were plastered and painted with frescoes, little trace of which remains today.

Perhaps the most finely executed and best-preserved sculpture of a descending god at Tulúm is on Structure 25,

The structure called the Castillo, with its back to the sea, domi-
nates the site of Tulúm. On each side of the staircase is a small
oratory structure used by the Maya priests. The Castillo may
have been a temple-type structure. However, it does have addi-
tional rooms that may have housed the priests. All the structures
at Tulúm are a decadent Postclassic style. Toltec influence is
noted in the architecture.

located just north of the Temple of the Frescoes. The interlaced decorative detail on the sides of the god is especially
noteworthy. Some of the original color is still visible on this
deity.

To the southeast of the inner precinct is a building referred to as the Temple of the Initial Series. This building
originally housed a stela, found broken in pieces, that had a

date corresponding to A.D. 761. Since this is an "initial series" date, the structure was given its name from the stela. Knowing the building was constructed many centuries after this time, one can only guess that the stela was moved to Tulúm from some other ceremonial center. Now the stela is housed in the British Museum. The Temple of the Initial Series, as well as some other buildings at Tulúm, has walls punctuated by open windows. At one time the Temple of the Initial Series had a stucco façade, but little is here today to indicate the content or quality.

Should there be time at Tulúm to investigate a building outside the great wall, a hike some distance to the north will lead to Structure 59. This edifice is unique at Tulúm in having the only roof comb. The design of the roof comb is an open triangle arranged in a double row. Roof combs, used in many sites throughout the Mayan area, gave height and emphasis to building façades.

A pathway north of the Temple of the Descending God leads down the embankment to the sea. Today, as in the time when Tulúm was active, fishermen easily gather a plentiful catch of fish, lobsters, conches, and clams. The view along the coast is highlighted by rock outcroppings, stretches of white sand beaches, and the blue-green sea splashing against large rocks that have tumbled from the cliff into the water.

Tulúm lacks the refinement, beauty, and creative ingenuity of the work of earlier Mayan craftsmen. Nevertheless, there is a charm about it. The site imparts a sense of struggle and accomplishment. There is much to explore, to investigate, to search for in the diminutive style of architecture, which is such a change from other Mayan sites. The beauty of the spot, alone, is not easily forgotten. Tulúm stands today as a solitary buttress against the sea.

Suggestions for Reaching
Archaeological Zones

Pacific Slope: By private car. A knowledgeable guide from Guatemala City who is familiar with the *fincas* around the area of El Baúl and La Democracia would be advisable.

Iximché and Zaculeu: Both these sites can be reached by car from Guatemala City. For Iximché take the highway going toward Lake Atitlan and turn off for the village of Tecpan. Since the road is bad from this village to the ruins, a local bus can be used for this last 2 mile drive. For Zaculeu continue to Quetzeltenango and then proceed to Huehuetenango. Hotels are at both these communities. The drive from Huehuetenango to the Zaculeu ruins is only 2 miles. At Zaculeu there is also a small landing field for private aircraft.

Mixco Viejo: By car from Guatemala City. Be sure to check the conditions of the river crossing this side of Mixco Viejo. Sometimes the little bridge has been washed out. Should the river be impassable by car, the walk from the river to the ruins is approximately two miles.

Quiriguá: By car from Guatemala City. The trip can be made in one day. There are no accommodations at Quiriguá.

Copán: From Guatemala City it is possible to charter a private plane for Copán, but it is expensive. Occasionally planes are scheduled from Tegucigalpa in Honduras. A travel agent in Guatemala City may be of assistance in this type of arrangement. It is also possible to fly to San Pedro Sula from Guatemala City. At this point you can hire a car or take a local bus over the long, dusty road to San José de Copán. The ruins are only a mile from Copán village. Accommodations are available in the village.

Seibal: Plane from Guatemala City to Flores. At this point a four-wheel-drive vehicle is needed for the trip on the dirt road to Sayaxché and Seibal. You will have to cross the Pasión River on a ferry this side of Sayaxché. From Sayaxché the trip up the Pasión River is made by dugout canoe if the road is in poor condition, especially during the rainy season, or by vehicle if the condition of the rutted road to Seibal is satisfactory.

Tikal: Plane from Guatemala City to Tikal. During the rainy season flights can be irregular. A network of dirt roads connects Belize, Flores, San Pedro Sula, and Tikal, but the roads are not always passable because of the rains. Accommodations are available in Tikal.

Tulúm: A small landing field one mile from Tulúm is available for private planes from Mérida or Cozumel. It is possible to go by boat from the island of Cozumel to Tulúm, but weather conditions often make this trip impossible or unadvisable. A highway now is open from Mérida to Puerto Juárez, and it continues along the Caribbean coast to Tulúm. This trip can be made by private car and there are accommodations at Tancah—just north of Tulúm.

Chichén Itzá, Uxmal, and *Kabah:* Can easily be reached by car from Mérida, and accommodations are available.

Sayil, Xlapak, and Labná: By car from Mérida to Uxmal. At the Hacienda Uxmal arrangements can be made for transportation in a four-wheeled-drive vehicle from Uxmal to these remote sites. A competent guide who knows the unmarked trails through the jungle and who is familiar with the sites is necessary. The trip is not advisable during the rainy season.

Palenque: By scheduled airline from Mexico City or Mérida to Villahermosa. Transportation from Villahermosa to Palenque can be arranged by car. The drive is seventy miles. Accommodations are available in Palenque.

Yaxchilán and *Bonampak:* The easiest way to get to these remote sites is by private aircraft from Villahermosa or Palenque. The trip is made to both sites in the same day. There are no accommodations at either site. These sites can also be reached from Sayaxché by dugout canoe along the Usumacinta River. Overland hikes would then be necessary.

ORGANIZED TOURS

Organized tours are available to some of the archaeological ruins. These include Uxmal, Kabah, Labná, Sayil, Xlapak and Chichén Itzá in Yucatán. In Guatemala there are organized tours that go to Tikal. The other ruins require private car, plane, or train transportation "on your own." Local travel agencies in the Maya area can be especially helpful in arranging transportation with drivers. Arrangements also need to be made for competent guides.

A WORD ABOUT CLOTHING

Persons traveling to the Maya ruins should dress as casually and travel as light as possible. Slacks for both men and women are essential for most areas. Because of sunburn and in a few places insects, it is best to keep your arms and legs covered. Also a hat with a brim is necessary to shade the face. The tropical sun can give a very bad burn. Be sure to

321

include sun glasses and suntan lotion. Rubber-soled shoes with low heels or sneakers are a "must."

In the Guatemalan highlands, while visiting the sites of Zaculeu, Iximché, and Mixco Viejo, you should be prepared for cooler weather. Altitudes range from 4,500 to 6,500 feet and evenings can be chilly. A sweater or jacket can come in handy. At Copán, even though the altitude is only 2,000 feet, there are occasionally chilly nights. The tropical lowlands are hot and humid. For Tikal, Seibal, Palenque, Quiriguá, Bonampak and Yaxchilán, clothing should be light and washable. Shorts are not recommended here because of possible insects and the danger of sunburn. If you are allergic to insect bites, you should carry insect repellent.

In Yucatán and Quintana Roo the temperature is always hot, although drier than the tropical lowlands. Nights are somewhat cooler. Again light clothing is essential. Dinner dress at hotels is extremely casual. Dresses for women or jackets and ties for men are not necessary.

Laundry service is available only at Uxmal and Chichén Itzá, and you should allow two days for this service. There is no service at any of the other site accommodations. However, hotels in Guatemala City and Mérida have laundry service. A bathing suit will come in handy for those who enjoy swimming as pools are available at both Uxmal and Chichén Itzá.

During the rainy season, from May to December, a plastic raincoat is needed. In Yucatán the rainy season has many sunny days, and when rain does come, it is often a short shower followed by sunny skies. In the tropical lowlands in the Petén and along the Usumacinta and Motagua rivers, however, rain is more constant. The best time to visit the Maya area is from January to April, although travelers do make the trip throughout summer and fall.

Selected Readings

Benson, Elizabeth P. *The Maya World*. New York, 1967.

Coe, Michael D. *The Maya*. New York, 1966.

Coe, William R. *Tikal: A Handbook of the Ancient Maya Ruins*. Philadelphia, 1967.

Culbert, T. Patrick, ed. *The Classic Maya Collapse*. Albuquerque, 1973.

Greene, Merle. *Ancient Maya Relief Sculpture*. New York, 1967.

———. *Maya Sculpture*, Berkeley, 1972.

Kidder, Alfred V., Jesse L. Jennings, and Edwin M. Shook. *Excavations at Kaminaljuyú, Guatemala*, Carnegie Institution of Washington *Publ. 561*. Washington, D.C., 1946.

Kubler, George. *The Art and Architecture of Ancient America*. Baltimore, 1962.

Longyear, John M. "Copán Ceramics," Carnegie Institution of Washington *Publ. 597*. Washington, D.C., 1952.

Lothrop, Samuel K. *Tulúm: An Archaeological Study of the East Coast of Yucatán*, Carnegie Institution of Washington *Publ. 335*. Washington, D.C., 1924.

———, and others. *Essays in Pre-Columbian Art and Archaeology*. Cambridge, 1964.

Maudslay, Alfred P. *Archaeology. Biologia Centrali-Americana*. 5 vols. London, 1889–1902.

Morley, Sylvanus G. *The Ancient Maya*. 3rd ed. revised by G. W. Brainerd. Stanford, 1956.

———. *The Inscriptions of Petén*, Carnegie Institution of Washington *Publ. 435*. 5 vols. Washington, D.C., 1937–38.

Proskouriakoff, Tatiana. *An Album of Maya Architecture*, Carnegie Institution of Washington *Publ. 558*. Washington, 1946. Reprinted, Norman, 1963.

Recinos, Adrián. *Popol Vuh: The Sacred Book of the Ancient Quiché Maya.* Norman, 1950.
Robiscek, Francis. *Copán: Home of the Maya Gods.* New York. 1972.
Ruppert, Karl, J. Eric S. Thompson, and Tatiana Proskouriakoff, *Bonampak, Chiapas, Mexico,* Carnegie Institution of Washington *Publ.* 602. Washington, D.C., 1955.
Ruz L., Alberto. *The Civilization of the Ancient Maya.* Mexico, 1970.
Smith, A. Ledyard, and Alfred V. Kidder. *Excavations at Nebaj, Guatemala,* Carnegie Institution of Washington *Publ.* 594. Washington, D.C., 1951.
Spinden, Herbert J. *A Study of Maya Art, Memoirs* of the Peabody Museum of Archaeology and Ethnology, Harvard University, Vol. 6. Cambridge, 1913.
Stephens, John L. *Incidents of Travel in Central America, Chiapas, and Yucatan.* New York, 1841.
———. *Incidents of Travel in Yucatán.* New York, 1843. Reprinted, Norman, 1962.
Stone, Doris. *Pre-Columbian Man Finds Central America.* Cambridge, 1972.
Thompson, J. Eric S. *The Rise and Fall of the Maya Civilization.* Norman, 1954; 2nd edition, enlarged, 1966.
———. *Maya Hieroglyphic Writing.* Norman, 1960.
———. *Maya History and Religion.* Norman, 1970.
Wauchope, Robert, gen. ed. *Handbook of Middle American Indians.* Vols. II and III. Austin, Texas, 1965.
Woodbury, Richard B., and Aubrey Trik. *The Ruins of Zacaleu, Guatemala.* Boston, 1953.

Index

Acanceh, Mexico: 276, 278
Aguateca, Guatemala: 179
Ah Puch (god of death): 21
Altar de Sacrificios, Guatemala: 10,
    179, 181, 188, 190
Altars: 16, 49–52, 55, 66, 77, 88, 90,
    102, 106, 121–22, 295
Altun Ha, Belize: 19
Alvarado, Captain Pedro de: 196,
    208
Andesite: 11, 77–78
Annals of the Cakchiquels: 21
Archaeological zones: transportation
    and routes to, 319–20
Arches: 14, 144, 246; Labna Vault,
    270, 275, 304
Arroyo Yaxchilán: 158
Arts, the: 56, 112
Astronomy: 5–6, 16, 134; at Copán,
    6, 76, 106, 112; at Palenque, 135
Aztecs: 7, 38, 209–10, 216, 312;
    ball game, 98

Ball courts: 58–59, 76, 312; at
    Copán, 95, 98; Yaxchilán, 164;
    Zaculeu, 202; Mixco Viejo, 208,
    210; Chichén Itzá, 283–85
Ball games: 12, 37, 76, 95, 98, 284
Basel, Switzerland, museum in: 41
Bay of Campeche: 126
Bee Ruin, Mexico: 174
Belize: 5, 6
Belize River: 127
Bernoulli, Gustav: 41
Blom, Franz: 134
Bolivia: 154
Bonampak, Mexico: 6, 135; murals,
    20, 52, 66, 76, 106, 168, 174–78;
    ceremonial center, 127; location,

168–69; lintels, 172, 174; stelae,
    172, 174; Main Plaza, 172; stair-
    way, 174; Structure 1, 174, 177;
    glyphs, 174
Bourne, John: 172
British Museum: 318
Burials: 19, 52, 59, 67, 70; at
    Palenque, 148–50; Zaculeu, 202–
    203

Caibal Balam, Chief: 197
Calendrics: 16, 22, 226
Campeche, Mexico: 180
Caribbean islands: 216
Carnegie Institution of Washington:
    82, 283, 307
Catherwood, Frederick: 114, 306
Causeways: 66, 184, 256; *see also*
    highways
Cenotes: 12, 19, 221, 283, 289–91;
    see also Well of Sacrifice *and*
    Chichén Itzá
Central America: 154, 191, 221,
    306, 311; *see also* Mesoamerica
Ceramics: 18–19, 180, 211–13, 219
Ceremonial centers: 6, 10–12, 17,
    20, 24, 216, 256; at Copán, 14,
    76, 90, 127; maintenance, 18; in
    Postclassic period, 22–23; at Tikal,
    45, 67; Quiriguá, 114–15, 125,
    127; Yaxchilán, 127, 158, 168;
    Bonampak, 127; Uxmal, 223;
    Chichén Itzá, 278, 287, 291–92,
    294–95
Chac (rain god): 21, 229
Chamá, Guatemala: 18, 180, 202
Charnay, Désiré: 134, 158
Chavín culture: 3
Chavín de Huantar, Peru: 3

Chenes style (architecture): 226, 229, 256, 302
Chiapas, Mexico: 6, 11, 85, 126, 158, 168, 205
Chichén Itzá, Mexico: 19, 185, 226, 229, 256, 276, 279, 305, 307; Tzompantli, 185, 284, 287; Well of Sacrifice, 221, 283, 289–91; ceremonial center, 278, 287, 291–92, 294–95; and Toltecs, 278, 282, 287, 289; Castillo, 282, 284, 291, 294, 304; excavation, restoration, 283; ball courts, 283–85, 304; Temple of the Jaguars, 283–84; lintels, 283, 294, 302; Main Plaza, 284, 289; Platform of the Jaguar and Eagles, 287; Venus Platform, 287–89; Temple of the Warriors, 291–92, 294–95, 304; *chacmools*, 294; steam baths, 295–96; Caracol (observatory), 296–97, 302; Nunnery, 296, 302, 304; Iglesia, 296, 302; Red House, 296, 302; Temple of the Wall Panels, 302; *see also* Old Chichén
Cholula, Mexico: 5
Chultunes: 221, 275
Chimaltenango, Guatemala: 208, 213
Classic period: 5, 12, 18, 23, 38, 40–41, 48, 55, 60, 63, 70, 90, 125, 135, 143, 179–80, 185, 194, 196, 204, 216, 229, 256, 275, 287, 307, 311
Classic Veracruz era: 5, 10, 194, 204
Clothing for travel: 321–22
Cobá, Mexico: 11, 256
Coe, Michael: 310
Coe, William R.: 40, 49
Colombia: 125
Communication: 10–11, 126–27
Copán, Honduras: 5, 16, 18–19, 21, 52, 55, 91, 115–21, 125, 156, 188, 195, 202; astronomy, 6, 76, 106, 112; Hieroglyphic Stairway, 17, 88, 98–102, 112, 185; plaza, 74, 76, 82, 90, 95; ceremonial center, 74, 76, 90, 106, 112, 127; Hieroglyphic Court, 76, 88, 101; stelae, 76–77, 82–85, 88–90, 92, 95, 100, 106–107, 111–12, 148–49; glyphs, 77, 85, 88, 90, 92, 95, 98, 100–102, 145; altars, 77, 88, 90, 102, 106–107, 111; zoomorphs, 82, 88–90; abandoned, 90; Temple 11, 92, 101–102, 124; ball court, 95, 101; West Court, 102, 124; East Court, 106, 110; Acropolis, 106, 112; platforms, 110; Jaguar Stairway, 110; Temple 22, 210
Copán River: 106
Costa Rica: 5, 106, 112, 204, 289, 294
Cozumel, island of, Mexico: 22, 305
Crops: 11, 278
Cuernavaca, Mexico: 106

Diseases: 275
Doorways: 110, 124, 135–38, 148, 158, 162, 168, 174, 239, 246, 260–61, 271, 275, 283, 294; at Tulúm, 207, 311
Dos Pilas, Guatemala: 179
Dzibilchaltún, Mexico: 256, 276

Early Classic period: 45, 60, 188, 191, 198, 204, 276, 278
Early Postclassic period: 204, 278
Edzna, Mexico: 226, 283
Ek Chuah (god): 22
El Baúl, Guatemala: 31, 37
El Bilboa, Guatemala: 24, 31, 35–37, 39
El Caribe, Guatemala: 179
El Castillo, Guatemala: 31
El Salvador: 5, 6, 10, 24, 31, 38, 112, 191
El Tajín, Mexico: 7, 31, 204, 223, 312
El Transito, Guatemala: 24

Farming, slash-and-burn: 11, 70
Fincas: 24, 35–38

Finca San Francisco: *see* El Baúl
Flint: 11
Flores, Guatemala: 282
Frescoes: 6, 307, 312
Fretwork: 255, 265, 296
Friezes: 63, 154, 185, 233, 265, 273, 275, 284, 287–88, 304
Fry, H. Carl: 172

Gálvez, José Ricardo Muñoz: 36
Glyphs: 14–18; at Tikal, 52, 60; Copán, 77, 85, 88, 90, 92, 95, 98, 100–102; Yaxchilán, 145; Bonampak, 174; Seibal, 184–85; Uxmal, 253; *see also* hieroglyphics
Grijalva, Juan de: 305
Guatemala: 5, 6, 10, 24, 27, 29, 31, 37, 92, 114, 158, 196, 216, 287, 311
Guatemala City, Guatemala: 24, 38, 191, 194, 206, 208, 210
Guatemala highlands: 11, 19, 22, 38, 63, 114, 180, 190–91, 194, 203–204, 206

Hacienda Uxmal: 223
Harvard University: 179
Healey, Giles G.: 172
Hewett, Edgar L.: 115
Hieroglyphics: 14–17, 19; *see also* glyphs
Hieroglyphs: *see* glyphs
Highways: 11; *see also* causeways
Hochob, Mexico: 229
Honduras: 5, 6, 10–11, 31, 92, 114, 275
House of the Magician, Uxmal: 20, 226–33
House of the Three Lintels, Old Chichén: 265
Huehuetenango, Guatemala: 195
Huehuetenango Valley: 196

Incas: 7
Inscriptions of Petén, The: 158
Itzá family: 282, 311
Itzamná (Maya god): 22, 305

Ixchel (goddess): 22, 305
Iximché, Guatemala: 22, 208, 216; location, 217; ball courts, 217–18; Structure 2, 218–19; Temple II, 220; and human sacrifice, 220
Izamal, Mexico: 276, 278
Izapa, Mexico: 29

Jade: 11, 19, 59–60, 82, 84–85, 156, 180, 194, 205–206, 220, 282, 289; source of, 114, 204; in Palenque tomb, 149–50; at Zaculeu, 204
Jungle Lodge, Tikal: 40

Kabah, Mexico: 11, 195, 226, 304; causeway, 256; Palace of the Masks, 256–61; El Palacio, 261; El Columnas, 261
Kaminaljuyú, Guatemala: 10, 19, 24, 29, 38, 63, 114, 191, 196, 203–204; stone carvings, 194; artifacts, 194
Kelley, David: 116
Kinich Ahau (sun god): 22
Kubler, George: 239

Labná, Mexico: 195, 221, 233, 239, 261; Palace, 270–72; vault, 270, 275, 304; masks, 272–73; Castillo, 274–75
Lacanhá, Mexico: 172
Lacandon Indians: 169
La Democracía, Guatemala: 29
Lake Atitlán, Guatemala: 217
Lake Petén, Guatemala: 282
Landa, Bishop: 21
Las Ilusiones, Guatemala: 24, 31, 35
Late Classic period: 7, 12, 17, 19, 31, 35, 37, 41, 58–60, 63, 66–67, 106, 115, 120, 180, 190, 202–204, 216, 223, 229, 256, 278, 296, 304, 312
Late Postclassic period: 208, 213, 216, 220, 312
Late Preclassic period: 29, 188, 194
La Union, Honduras: 98
La Venta, Mexico: 27

Lhuillier, Alberto Ruz: 19, 134, 145, 148, 276
Limestone: 11, 119, 162, 172, 184
Lintels: 41, 59, 63, 158, 162, 164, 166–68, 172, 174, 246, 265, 271, 283, 294, 302
Los Tarros, Guatemala: 24, 31

Maler, Teobert: 41, 158, 179
Manzanal, Guatemala: 204
Masks: stucco, 49, 110, 172, 223, 265, 272–73, 294, 304; jade, 150; stone, 229, 255–61
Mathematics: 5, 134
Maudslay, Alfred: 41, 114–15, 134, 158
Maudslay, Mexico: 174
Maya Classic period: 311
Maya History and Religion: 7
Mayapán, Mexico: 22, 311
Mayas, the: 3, 37–38, 91–92, 125, 168, 178, 191, 202, 208, 296–97, 312; rise and fall of, 5–7, 10–12, 23, 216; culture, 10–19, 21–22, 106, 112, 135; architecture, 14, 17, 20, 45–48, 63, 74, 134, 156–57, 216, 239, 254, 261, 304; calendrics, 16, 22, 226, 310; codices, 17, 21; religion, 21–22, 88–89, 216, 304–305, 310–12; mythology, 38–39, 310; and human sacrifice, 52, 203; and class society, 67; life style, 70, 213; and symbolism, 122–24; communication, 10–11, 126–27; trade routes, 206; and internal strife, 213, 216–17; lineage, 217; *chultunes,* 221
Mérida, Mexico: 221, 223, 278–79
Mesoamerica: 3, 5, 20, 27, 41, 55, 66, 100, 150, 168, 204, 218, 220, 226, 283–84, 289, 311; *see also* Central America
Metates: 38, 220
Mexican highlands: 5, 38, 112, 278
Mexico: 5, 29, 31, 37, 63, 126, 158, 168, 213, 217, 221, 287, 311

Mexico City, Mexico: 5, 233
Middle Classic period: 31, 35, 121
Middle Preclassic period: 3, 14, 66, 188, 194
Miguel Angel Fernández, Mexico: 134, 172
Milpa farming: see slash-and-burn farming
Mitla, Mexico: 223
Mixco Viejo, Guatemala: 22, 206, 220, 311; military fortress, 208; platforms, 208, 210; ball courts, 208, 210; destruction, 208; architecture, 209; twin temples, 210; ceremonial center, 210; walls, 211; ceramics, 211–13
Mixtec codices: 219, 312
Mixtecs: 38, 219–20, 223
Moctezuma: 216
Monte Albán, Mexico: 5, 14, 150, 220, 255
Monte Alto, Guatemala: 24, 29, 31
Monuments: 6, 14, 16, 21, 37, 48, 74, 95; at Copán, 77–85, 88–90, 92; Quiriguá, 115–20, 122–24; Yaxchilán, 164; Seibal, 188; *see also* stelae
Morley, Sylvanus G.: 41, 115, 134, 158, 172, 179, 275, 312
Morris, E. H.: 115
Mosaics, stone: 6, 17, 125, 203–204, 223, 226, 275, 302
Motagua River: 112, 114, 204, 208
Mounds: 24, 37, 39, 115, 134, 158, 166, 188
Murals: 11, 18, 219, 284, 307, 310–13; at Bonampak, 20, 52, 66, 76, 106, 168, 174–78; Uaxactún, 76
Museum of Anthropology, Mexico City: 149, 295
Museo d'Homme, Paris, France: 211

National Institute of Anthropology and History of Mexico, Mexico City: 307
Nebaj, Guatemala: 19, 196, 203–

204; burials, 206; similarity to Zaculeu, 206
Nicoya Peninsula, Costa Rica: 106
Numerals: 85

Oaxaca, Mexico: 10, 289
Obsidian: 11, 180, 220
Ojos de Agua, Mexico: 172
Old Chichén, Mexico: 265, 295; House of the Three Lintels, 303–304; see also Chichén Itzá
Olmecs: 3, 27, 66, 90, 121; sites, 14, 27
Ortiz, Antonio: 40, 66
Oxlahuntún, Mexico: 172

Paintings, wall: 6, 17, 145, 316
Palaces: 18, 63, 135, 143–44, 146, 148, 265, 270
Palenque, Mexico: 5, 14, 49, 85, 88, 106, 126, 162, 164, 185, 195, 205; glyph panels, 16–17, 149, 154–56; Temple of the Inscriptions, 19, 52, 134, 145, 148–50; ceremonial center, 127, 135, 155; architecture, 134–36, 156–57; palaces, 135, 143–44, 146, 148; astronomy, 135; stucco decoration, 138, 142–43, 145, 149, 156; East Court, 144–45; carvings, 145; West Court, 145; glyphs, 145; steam bath, 145; tomb, 148–50; Temple of the Sun, 154–55; Temple of the Foliated Cross, 154–55; aqueduct, 155; Northern Group, 155–56; Temple of the Count, 155–56
Palenque (village), Mexico: 127
Panama: 125, 204, 289
Pantaleón, Guatemala: 24, 31
Parsons, Lee: 31, 37
Pasión River: 10, 127, 179, 216, 287
Pasión Valley: 184
Peabody Museum, Cambridge, Mass.: 100, 289
Pennsylvania, University of: 41, 70, 72
Peru: 3, 154

Petén region, Guatemala: 5, 10–12, 40–41, 55, 73, 127, 146, 202, 223, 229, 275, 311
Piedras Negras, Guatemala: 16, 106, 119, 162, 164, 172, 179, 188, 195, 229; ceremonial center, 127
Pipils: 7, 31
Plaques: 203
Platforms: 12, 124, 164, 166, 208, 210, 287–89
Plazas: 14, 45, 49, 55, 60, 63, 74, 76, 82, 90, 95, 115, 124, 164, 284, 289
Pocomam Mayas: 208
Postclassic period: 22–23, 38, 58, 100, 191, 196, 203–204, 210, 213, 217, 220, 223, 255, 287, 289, 304–305, 307, 310–11
Potrero Nuevo, Mexico: 295
Pottery: 11, 18, 21, 31, 55, 67, 88, 156, 194, 202, 216, 264, 289, 296, 304; Plumbate, 204; sherds, 307
Preclassic period: 12, 16–17, 38, 40, 45, 60, 116, 191, 194, 229, 255, 264, 276, 278, 307
Proskouriakoff, Tatiana: 6, 85
Proto Classic era: 29
Puerto Juárez, Mexico: 296
Puuc Hills, Mexico: 6, 164, 195, 221, 226, 242, 254, 256, 265, 270, 273
Puuc style (architecture): 226, 265, 302, 304
Pyramids: 5, 12, 45, 154

Quintana Roo, Mexico: 22, 305
Quiriguá, Guatemala: 16, 88, 90, 92, 95, 98, 112, 114, 127, 188, 195; ceremonial center, 114–15, 125; monuments, 115–20, 122–24; stelae and zoomorphs, 115–22, 125; plaza, 115, 124; glyphs, 116, 120–22, 124, 145; platform, 124; stairways, 124, 185
Quiriguá (village), Guatemala: 114

Rain forests: 112, 125, 168, 179

Ratinlixul, Guatemala: 18, 180, 202
Relación de las cosas de Yucatán:
    21
Río Bec: 226
Río Selegua: 196
Roof combs: 17, 45, 143–44, 162,
    166, 198, 246, 260, 275, 296, 318
Roofs, mansard-type: 143, 226
Ruins of Zaculeu, Guatemala, The:
    196
Ruppert, Karl: 172

Salina River: 179
Sandstone: 11, 119
San José de Copán, Honduras: 74
San Lorenzo, Mexico: 27
Santa Rita, Guatemala: 31
Santa Rita de Corozal, Belize: 312
Sayil, Mexico: 195, 221, 287, 304;
    Palace, 261–65, 270–71; lintels,
    265
Sculptures: 7, 24–26, 35–39, 52, 55,
    76–77, 82–85, 88–92, 115, 144,
    216, 219, 304; boulder, 29; Izapa
    style, 29, 31, 194; Cotzumalhuapa
    style, 31, 35, 37–38; mushroom
    stones, 38–39
Seibal, Guatemala: 10, 179; trade
    center, 180–81; stelae, 184–85,
    188; courtyards, plazas, 184–85;
    ball court, 184; Structure A-3,
    184–85; glyphs, 184–85; hiero-
    glyphic stairway, 185; Structure
    14, 185; monuments, 188, 190;
    mounds, 188; abandoned, 188,
    190
Seler, Eduard G.: 134
Shook, Edwin: 29
Smith, A. Ledyard: 179
Spaniards: 6, 17, 219, 282, 296, 305
Spanish Conquest: 23, 66, 191, 196,
    198–202, 206, 208, 213, 220
Spinden, Herbert: 158
Stairways: 17, 55, 74, 88, 92, 98–
    102, 110, 112, 124, 135, 162,
    166, 185, 263, 282–83, 294
Statues, dedicatory: see stelae

Steam baths: 145, 295–96
Stelae: 6, 16, 31, 37, 156, 184–85,
    188, 226, 287, 317–18; at Tikal,
    49–52; Copán, 76–77, 82–85, 88,
    90–92, 95, 100, 106–107, 111–12;
    Quiriguá, 115–22; Yaxchilán, 158,
    162; Bonampak, 172, 174; see also
    sculpture
Stephens, John L.: 114, 134, 306
Stone reliefs: 162, 164, 172, 174,
    194
Stromsvik, Gustav: 115
Stucco reliefs: 5, 12, 48–49, 134,
    138, 145, 149, 156, 162, 174, 177,
    185, 198, 223, 278, 312, 315

Tabasco: 6, 11, 14, 27, 126
Tarascans: 38
Tararindito, Guatemala: 179
Tecpán, Guatemala: 217, 219
Temple of the Inscriptions,
    Palenque: 19, 52, 134, 145,
    148–50
Temple of the Inscriptions, Tikal:
    52, 66
Temple of the Jaguar Priest, Tikal:
    60
Temples: 5–6, 12, 18, 21, 45, 52,
    55, 58–60, 92, 101–102, 110, 134,
    148–50, 154–56, 283–84, 291–92,
    294–95, 302, 304, 312–18
Tenochtitlán, Mexico: 287
Teotihuacán, Mexico: 5, 7, 10, 31,
    41, 63, 204, 276, 295
Thompson, Edward: 134, 282–83,
    289, 302
Thompson, J. Eric S.: 7, 154, 311
Tierra del Fuego, Chile: 3
Tikal, Guatemala: 4–5, 10–12, 16,
    19, 31, 40, 146, 184, 205; North
    Acropolis, 20, 45, 48–49, 52, 55,
    278; Central Acropolis, 40, 45,
    60–63; urban center, 41; excava-
    tion and reconstruction, 41–45,
    66, 70–72; ceremonial center, 45,
    67; Temple IV, 45, 52, 55, 59,
    282; roof combs, 45, 49, 55, 66;

Temples I and II, 45, 55, 58–60; plaza, 45, 49, 55, 60, 63; Temple V, 49, 55; stelae, 49–52, 66; Temple of the Inscriptions, 52, 66; Temple III, 52, 55, 59–60; burials, 52, 59, 67, 70; stairway, 55, 58; pyramids, 55, 58, 66, 73; lintels, 59–60, 63; "Maler Palace," 63; causeways, 66; and jungle area, 73
Tikal: A Handbook of the Ancient Maya Ruins: 40
Tikal Museum: 40, 59
Toltec-Maya style (architecture): 278
Toltecs: 7, 209, 278–79, 282, 287, 289, 291–92, 294–97, 302, 304, 311–12
Toniná, Mexico: 205
Tours, organized: 321
Tozzer, A. M.: 158
Tres Zapotes, Mexico: 27, 31, 121, 150
Trik, Aubrey S.: 196
Tula, Mexico: 210, 278, 282–83, 287, 292, 294–95; Pyramid of Quetzalcóatl, 291, 295
Tulúm, Mexico: 22, 265; ceremonial center, 305–306, 310, 318; walled, 306–307, 310; Castillo, 307, 310–11, 316; urban center, 310; Temple of the Initial Series, 310, 317–18; Temple of the Descending God, 310, 316–18; Temple of the Frescoes, 312–17
Tzendales, Mexico: 172

Uaxactún, Guatemala: 12, 76, 184, 229
Ulua River: 112
United Fruit Company: 114–16, 196
Usumacinta region: 85, 275, 311
Usumacinta River: 10, 127, 158, 162, 164, 166, 168, 172, 179, 206, 223
Uxmal, Mexico: 11, 14, 49, 195, 221, 256, 304–305, 307; House of the Magician, 20, 226–33, 255; ceremonial center, 223; mosaics, 223, 226; Pyramid of the Old Woman, 226; Nunnery, 233–39, 242–43, 255; ball court, 239; Palace of the Governor, 239, 254–55, 262; House of the Doves, 242–46, 249; lintels, 246; Grand Pyramid, 246–49; Cemetery Group, 249–54; House of the Turtles, 254, 304; abandoned, 255

Valley of Mexico: 7, 10, 216
Valley of Oaxaca, Mexico: 10
Vaults, vaulting: 14, 58, 135–38, 145, 246
Veracruz, Mexico: 3, 5, 10, 14, 27, 29, 31, 90, 121, 223
Volkerkunde Museum, Berlin, Germany: 37

Waldeck, Frederick: 134, 155–56
Well of Sacrifice, Chichén Itzá: 221, 283, 289–91; *see also cenotes and Chichén Itzá*
Willey, Gordon R.: 179
Woodbury, Richard B.: 196

Xanam Ik (god): 22
Xiu family: 255
Xlapak, Mexico: 261, 265, 304
Xochicalco, Mexico: 106

Yaxchilán, Mexico: 49, 88, 106, 127, 135, 179, 185, 195; glyphs, 145, 164, 166, 168; location, 158; lintels, 158, 162, 164, 166–68, 172, 174; ceremonial center, 127, 158, 168; stelae, altars, 158, 162, 166, 168; Main Plaza, 159, 164; monuments, 164; stone carvings, 162, 164; platforms, 164, 166; ball courts, 164; Structure 33, 164–66; South Acropolis, 166; West Acropolis, 166
Yaxhá, Guatemala: 66
Yaxuná, Mexico: 11, 256

Yucatán, Mexico: 5, 6, 22, 70, 164, 190, 195, 221, 223, 226, 246, 256, 275–76, 278, 283, 304–305, 307, 311–12
Yucatán Peninsula, Mexico: 6, 10–11, 276, 287, 289
Yum Kaax (maize god) : 21

Zaculeu, Guatemala: 180, 195–96, 213, 220; location, 196; house mounds, 196; ceremonial center restoration, 197–98; Structure 1, 198; Structure 4, 198; Structure 13, 198–99; ball court, 202; burials, 202–204; plaques, 203; mosaics, 203–204
Zapotec region: 10
Zoomorphs: 82, 88–90, 115–22

The paper on which this book is printed bears the watermark of the University of Oklahoma Press and has an effective life of at least three hundred years.